A History by Paul Carter

Capital Transport

First published 1995

ISBN 185414 173 2

Published by Capital Transport Publishing
38 Long Elmes, Harrow Weald, Middlesex

Printed by Portswood Colour Press Ltd
Central Trading Estate, Southampton

CONTENTS

6 **The Background and the Beginning** (1932-1939)

12 **Wartime** (1939-1945)

16 **The Great Expansion** (1945-1950)

38 **More Growth in Difficult Times** (1951-1955)

46 **Out of the Wood** (1956-1959)

54 **Celebration, New Coaches, One-Man Buses** (1960-1964)

66 **Coach Expansion, Rural Decline** (1965-1970)

80 **Bus Grant, New Image** (1971-1975)

90 **Fleet Standardisation** (1976-1980)

94 **The Age of the Coach** (1980-1985)

106 **Bus Deregulation** (1986-1987)

114 **The AJS Era: New Beginnings** (1988-1990)

128 **List of Vehicles Owned**

Front cover, upper photo by Paul Carter
Front cover, lower photo by Geoff Rixon
Back cover photos supplied by Cambridge Coach Services Ltd

AUTHOR'S NOTE

I first noticed the buses of Premier Travel in Cambridge during the early 1950s. Over the next few years I was occasionally surprised to find them at work in various out-of-the-way places, although I rarely travelled on them until the late 1960s. By then I had begun to appreciate how important they were to many rural communities scattered over a wide area, where the arrival of the blue bus was part of a well-ordered routine. The bus was very much a meeting place for the local people with their regular travelling habits, and a loyal following was built up. The absence of a passenger on an inward journey could result in serious consultations between passengers and crew as the bus waited at an isolated farm or cottage. A missing regular on the return journey could also cause a delay until the latecomer was safely on board. The long-established routes adequately served the local community, taking people to the towns for the markets and relaxation, and sometimes to work on the daily services, of which there were several. Pleasure traffic was also catered for by the 'picture buses' which were operated for many years. Cambridge once had eight cinemas, with at least one in each of the market towns. Most have now closed, victims of television, although Cambridge still has two and that at Royston happily survives. In the heyday of the cinema, late-night buses waited for programmes to end before departing to the villages, often with standing loads. In Bishop's Stortford the bus crews were allowed to watch the films on offer before the late departures on Services 10 and 26. Both of these required a double-decker, sometimes with a 20-seater from Stort Taxis as a relief for the first part of the journey.

Extra buses also ran for special events, such as the fairs at Royston, Huntingdon and St Ives, while the townspeople could (and did) use the blue buses to reach the countryside. In the early 1950s Service 56 even had a special Boxing Day journey from and to Haverhill "...to the Meet of the Newmarket and Thurlow Hounds". The post-war boom on the local bus routes was short-lived, however. Some services were never busy, and loadings on others declined slowly during the 1950s, and much more rapidly during the 1960s as car ownership increased; this happened faster in East Anglia than almost anywhere else. Subsidies from County Councils ensured the survival of some routes, but the payments came too late to help the whole network. Large-scale cuts were necessary, and on the surviving services frequencies were often greatly reduced.

As the bus network withered, the long-distance express operations grew, helped by the decline of cross-country rail services. Some Saturdays-only services were increased to run on Sundays as well, then additionally on Fridays and Mondays. Eventually a daily service would be introduced, initially only in the summer but finally on an all-year-round basis. The same customer loyalty was built up as on the bus services, and this was still evident in later days when Premier Travel and National Express offered alternative services to the same destinations. Regular travellers returned each year and were adamant that it was the Premier service that they wished to travel on; some would depart for their annual holiday year after year with the same driver in charge of the coach. The express operations steadily developed into a successful network of daily services, and several of the expresses started by Premier Travel run to this day.

The Duple-bodied Dennis Lancet coaches were once the pride of the coach fleet. This vehicle was the last Dennis to be purchased new and was photographed a few years later taking part in the first British Coach Rally on April 17th 1955. This event took place in Clacton, where Premier Travel coaches were already a familiar sight. The Lancets were featured in company publicity material for many years, this coach lasting until 1964. *J C Gillham*

I became part of Premier Travel in 1972, when I joined the company as a part-time conductor. Life was much more hectic (but just as enjoyable) in the Drummer Street office, after which I went back on the road as a driver. Returning to Cambridge in the summer of 1990, I was immediately aware of a gap in the local transport scene following the division and sale of the company I knew so well. This book tells the story of an independent enterprise, which was begun by enthusiastic amateurs in a world very different from today's, when changes took place slowly and the pace of life was far more gentle. I wish to acknowledge the help and encouragement I have received from many people, notably Mr & Mrs E A Lainson, Frank Matthews, Jack and Maisie Gifford, Jeff Aldous, Roger Birch, Geoff Bray, Geoff Cochrane, John Gower, Frank Grice, Basil and Kit Holmes, David Hurry, Mike Northfield, Ian Roberts, Reg Roope, Andrew Weir and Ken Worland (all formerly with Premier Travel); Peter Andrews and Margaret Camp of Premier Travel Holdings; Annette for all her support; Mike Fenton and Brian Parkin for information on Wilks & Meade; Peter Clark, the staff of the Cambridgeshire Collection at Cambridge Central Library and all the photographers who allowed their work to be included, especially Geoff Mills (who also helped with the fleet list) and Colin Routh.

Wadhurst, East Sussex, December 1994   PAUL CARTER

FLEET NUMBERING: Throughout the text I have referred to vehicles by their registration numbers. Although fleet numbers were carried, they were often subject to change and, throughout my time with Premier, vehicles were identified by the figures of the registration number; thus DCK212 was '212' or maybe 'DD 212'. It carried fleet number 138, but few staff would have known which bus was being referred to had this number been mentioned.

CHAPTER ONE

THE BACKGROUND AND THE BEGINNING
1932-1939

By 1930 the University city of Cambridge was well served by rail, bus and express coach services. Most of the country buses used the Drummer Street terminus which came into use in 1925, and there were many operators providing services. The largest was the Ortona Motor Company Ltd, with nearly 100 double- and single-deck vehicles on town and country services. Buses of the large Eastern National company also appeared, while the other operators were small, village-based concerns. Of these the only survivor is Whippet Coaches, now based at Fenstanton to the north of the city. The others have all vanished, among them Burwell & District, Brand of Elsworth, Cambridge Blue of Arrington, Comfort & Reliance of Cottenham, Drayton of Barley, Fenstanton & District, Francis of Quy, Long of West Wratting, Thompson of Harston and Weeden of Chrishall. Apart from the bus services there were also express coaches to London, either via Ware, or Bishop's Stortford. These were operated by Varsity Express Motors Ltd and the associated Varsity Coaches Ltd, based in Cambridge and London. Express services to seaside resorts were also provided by several operators.

The 1930 Road Traffic Act eliminated some of the fierce competition which existed between rival operators. The Act required each individual service to have a Road Service Licence, and operators had to prove a demand for services before the Traffic Commissioners would grant licences. Public Service Vehicle licences were introduced for vehicles, drivers and conductors, and the once-familiar PSV badges had to be worn by crews. Soon after the Act was passed several local firms disappeared. In July 1931 Ortona was amalgamated with three other large East Anglian operators to form the Eastern Counties Omnibus Co Ltd. The new company's red and cream livery replaced Ortona's green, and Eastern Counties set about acquiring smaller operators throughout its territory. Over the next few years it absorbed Comfort & Reliance and both Varsity businesses.

It was against this background of regulation and change that interesting events were taking place in an unexpected quarter, namely St Catherine's College. The players were ten young gentlemen led by Mr E A Lainson, a Suffolk man and a lifelong transport enthusiast. The undergraduates (they were not usually called 'students' in those far-off days) had become bored by study and sport, and they decided to start a bus company. Having each contributed £5 in capital, they designated themselves as Directors, and registered their company under the Business Names Act as Undergraduate Roadways. They took their venture quite seriously, despite the fact that they were running a bus company with no buses. This was solved by operating on the 'Permit to Hire' basis: established local operators were engaged to do private hire jobs which Undergraduate Roadways had obtained at a slightly lower rate than the operators' own quotations. Representatives were appointed in other colleges, and Undergraduate Roadways handled a number of private hires, using vehicles from Comfort & Reliance, Drayton's, Varsity and Weeden's. Unfortunately the enterprise soon came to the attention of the college authorities. They did not approve of a commercial venture being carried on by undergraduates, whose names were accordingly removed from company stationery. The 'offices' moved to a new address outside the University, although operations continued. Encouraged by their success, the young gentlemen decided in 1933 to start a regular, timetabled service. Weekend trips to the seaside were popular, although the nearest resorts already had services from Cambridge. Looking further afield, the Directors hit upon the idea of a Cambridge - Peterborough - Skegness service. They worked out a timetable, sent off their application and appointed an enthusiastic young solicitor to represent them at the Traffic Courts. Witnesses were needed to prove that a demand existed, and the Directors visited the Dean of Peterborough Cathedral, pointing out that the service would enable people to attend services at the cathedral more easily. Support was also forthcoming from three operators who were willing to provide vehicles. It was necessary to apply for licences in the Eastern and the East Midland Traffic Areas, and objections were received from several coach operators in the East Midlands, as well as from Eastern Counties and the London & North Eastern Railway Company. In spite of these, and to the delight of all concerned, the licences were granted and the service duly commenced. Departing from Cambridge at 9am on Sundays and Bank Holidays, it travelled via Peterborough, Market Deeping, Spalding, Gosberton and Wrangle, arriving in the early afternoon at Skegness, described in publicity as "The Finest Resort on the East Coast" with "every conceivable amenity". All journeys were operated by Varsity Express Motors, working 'On Hire to Undergraduate Roadways'.

Mr Lainson obtained his degree in 1934 and 'went down'. He tried to find himself a position in the bus and coach industry, but the Depression was at its height and no suitable opening presented itself. He therefore decided once again to start his own company, this time by taking over and expanding the services of established local concerns. He visited numerous operators on his bicycle, but only two expressed any real interest; these were N C P Thompson of Harston (operating as 'Harston & District') and H J Brown of Cambridge ('Royal Blue Coaches'), both of whom had commenced operations soon after the First World War.

Mr Lainson also advertised in the technical press for investors for his new venture, and the eventual outcome was the formation in January 1936 of Premier Travel Ltd, with a registered office at 15 Market Hill, Cambridge. The Chairman was Sir Christopher Magnay Bart, MC, who had been a Director of the Premier Omnibus Company Ltd in London before Premier's services were compulsorily taken over by the London Passenger Transport Board. With the backing of Sir Christopher and his associate Captain C G P Kirk, together with some additional capital from Mr Lainson himself, the new company took over the operations of Harston & District and Royal Blue. Mr Thompson continued for a while as a Director of Premier Travel, and Mr Lainson was initially Company Secretary. In the meantime Undergraduate Roadways (which had continued to function within the University) was finally wound up in 1935, when Mr Lainson acquired the remaining shareholdings and incorporated it into Premier Travel as a subsidiary company.

One of the original vehicles acquired at the start of operations, this Gilford AS6 is seen here in its original livery, complete with Harston & District fleetname and 'NT' (for Norman Thompson) monogram. It had a 20-seat body of unknown manufacture and lasted until September 1944. Visible in the background is Reo VE3002, which was also taken over. The Harston & District routes became Premier Travel Services 1 and 2, and for many years terminated at the Green Man in Royston, on a section of road which is now one-way in the opposite direction. *J F Higham*

Two other Gilford coaches were taken over with the Harston & District operations. This one had a Beadle 30-seat body and is seen in Drummer Street, Cambridge on Service 2 to Barrington. The Gilfords were expensive to maintain and difficult to drive, but others followed and there were six in the fleet by autumn 1939. This one survived the war and was withdrawn in July 1945. *R F Mack*

The vehicles acquired from Harston & District and Royal Blue were a motley assortment which needed a great deal of maintenance to keep them going. Four different makes of chassis were represented by six small buses and coaches: Harston & District initially provided a Reo (VE3002) and three Gilfords (VE4993, VE8761 and WG334). From Royal Blue came an Associated Daimler (YE4390) which had started life with the London General Omnibus Company, and a Maudslay (VE919). Both the acquired operators had used blue-based liveries, and the vehicles were now repainted in the smart and unusual livery of two shades of blue adopted by their new owner. The lighter shade was officially known as 'Premier blue' and was mixed to special order.

The six vehicles worked from the former Harston & District depot in the village of that name to the south of Cambridge. The local bus services continued to operate between Cambridge and Royston. Service 1 followed a roundabout route through Haslingfield and the villages of Newton, Thriplow and Fowlmere on the Old London Road (now the B1368) while Service 2 served Barrington. There was competition with the Cambridge - Royston routes of Eastern Counties (Service 108) and Eastern National (Service 41), and to strengthen their position these companies proposed ticket interavailability on each other's buses. This was naturally opposed by Premier Travel, who wanted to co-ordinate its fares with those of the larger operators, although this was not agreed until many years later. The larger operators also (unsuccessfully) objected to Premier's application to divert Service 2 via Hauxton Village.

Coaching consisted of contracts, private hires and the summer express services, for which extra vehicles had to be hired to cope with the loadings. The Cambridge to Skegness route became Service 3, while Service 4 was the former Royal Blue operation from Cambridge direct to Great Yarmouth. Royal Blue had also operated the May Races service referred to on page 53. Despite shortages of staff and the make-do-and-mend nature of the fleet, the new company set about improving the depot and building up operations. Further expansion was considered in May 1936, when the possible takeover of Weeden's of Chrishall was discussed. Lack of capital prevented this for the time being, but further meetings followed with Weeden's, and other operators.

It was decided that new coaches were essential if Premier was to have a first-class fleet, and the company proudly purchased its first new vehicle at the end of 1936. This was BVE668, a Bedford WTB with a Duple 25-seat coach body, for which the Maudslay was part-exchanged. The Associated Daimler was also withdrawn, eliminating the ex-Royal Blue vehicles after only a year with their new owner.

The first new vehicle to be purchased by Premier Travel was this Bedford WTB, which arrived in December 1936. It was the first of several Bedford/Duple coaches, and it lasted in the fleet until 1952, when it was sold for scrap. The only known photograph of the coach shows it at Drummer Street in 1947. *G R Mills collection*

Another Gilford joined the fleet in March of the following year; this was WG1284 which like WG334 had first seen service in Scotland in the Alexander fleet. An additional Reo from Harston & District (VE855) was also licensed by Premier Travel for the first time, and to save on operating costs it had its seating reduced from 26 to 20 so that it could operate without a conductor. This left a seatless area in the middle of the vehicle with nothing for standing passengers to hang on to, and it was rather hazardous to ride in.

Mr Lainson had already recognised the potential of long-distance express services, and his declared ambition was to have a network of coaches throughout the country. A very significant development in that direction took place in April 1937, when Premier Travel purchased the licence for one of its most important routes. Service 5 (as it became) was previously operated by the old-established Webber Brothers ('Empire's Best') of Wood Green, London. It linked Birmingham, Coventry and Leicester with Colchester and Clacton via Northampton, Bedford and Cambridge and ran three times a week. The service became increasingly busy after Premier Travel took over, and it has often been said that the licence for it (which cost £505) was the best purchase the company ever made. Additional routes were planned from the Midlands and the north to the Essex coast. In an attempt to safeguard its position, Premier also opposed (unsuccessfully) an application by Allenways of Birmingham for a Birmingham - Dovercourt summer service.

Another new coach arrived in May 1937, in the form of a splendid Dennis Lancet (CCE568). Like the Bedford, it compared very favourably with the older Gilfords. The design of the latter vehicles owed much to American influence, and as well as being expensive to maintain they were rather noisy. Their gear levers also became very hot after a while, which made changing up or down (already quite an art) even more of a problem for the drivers.

The company had a busy year in 1937. Apart from its new express service, and an increase in private hire revenue, there was also a strike by Eastern Counties crews which went on for several weeks. The Directors made it clear that they did not wish to take sides in the dispute, but felt that passenger numbers would only be maintained if services continued to be provided. It was proposed that Premier should operate between Cambridge and Royston via the main road and also on Eastern Counties 104 (Cambridge - Cottenham). Eastern Counties would not agree to the latter proposal, but loadings increased steadily on the Royston road, and passenger loyalty improved as a result.

The two Reos were withdrawn early in 1938, and a six-year lifespan for vehicles was proposed. This was not to be, for there were now financial difficulties. Despite Mr Lainson's boundless enthusiasm and an apparently successful year, debts had built up. A trading loss of £460 was recorded for 1937, and Premier Travel almost came to an early end. Sir Christopher Magnay resigned, recommending that the firm go into voluntary liquidation. Captain Kirk also withdrew, leaving Mr Lainson (who became Chairman) and Mr Thompson to effect an improvement, or go under.

As Europe headed for war, Premier Travel's performance improved steadily. Two more secondhand Gilfords were purchased; HX3464 arrived in June 1938 from Crouch End Luxury Coaches, followed in June 1939 by TM8465. This had started life with Strawhatter Motor Coaches of Luton and later passed to Eastern National, but Premier Travel bought it for £50 from a travelling salesman. It had a habit of lurching forward when starting, and soon acquired the nickname 'Tom Mix'.

The 1937 Dennis Lancet was larger than the Bedford, with 35 seats in its opulently-styled Duple body, and it served its owners faithfully for 20 years. Passengers travelling to and from the north on Service 5 were treated to the famous view in Cambridge of King's College Chapel from The Backs, but for many years Service 5 avoided Drummer Street, calling instead at The Spread Eagle in Lensfield Road on the edge of the city centre. This arrangement continued until 1963. *Courtesy M J Gifford*

The summer of 1939 was a particularly good one, with people determined to enjoy themselves before the inevitable happened. The express services carried especially healthy loads, right up to the declaration of war in September. By that time Premier Travel was running a fleet of eight vehicles, consisting of the nearly-new Bedford and Dennis (BVE668 and CCE568) together with six second-hand Gilfords.

CHAPTER TWO
WARTIME
1939-1945

The summer came to an abrupt end in September 1939, and the atmosphere changed immediately. Many new regulations came into force, among them restrictions on vehicle lighting. Headlamps had to be masked and interior lighting reduced, making life difficult for crews. Wartime transport became a priority; on one occasion the entire fleet was ordered to Cambridge railway station to help with the movement of evacuees. The flat East Anglian terrain was ideal for the siting of aerodromes, and the Royal Air Force was already well-established in the area. Troops needed transport, and carrying airmen and aircraft fitters became an important part of operations. The general public also had to make "really necessary" journeys, and the buses on Services 1 and 2 were often very crowded. The express services were withdrawn, although discussions took place with Midland Red in November to plan a limited coastal service for munitions workers in the summer of 1940. Nothing came of this, and in any case much of Britain's coastline was by then "out of bounds".

Everything seemed to be in short supply, and exhortations to salvage and recycle were everywhere. A passenger who examined the reverse side of his bus ticket would be encouraged to "...Help US to help YOU. Travel midweek when you can. REMEMBER. Petrol & Spares are needed for the War Effort".

Several of the staff joined the armed forces, as indeed did Mr Lainson, even though transport management was a reserved occupation. Mr Thompson found himself back in charge of operations, assisted now by Mrs Lainson. Life was far from easy, for although the company's financial position had improved by 1939, the withdrawal of the express services (particularly Service 5) led to a serious drop in revenue. The lack of staff, spare parts and money began to cause serious difficulties, and consideration was given to the idea of selling the Service 5 licence and closing the Cambridge office. The Dennis (CCE568) was requisitioned by the RAF and suffered engine failure on its return. Its engine was dismantled, but nothing more was done. Maintenance and servicing became increasingly erratic, as the fitters kept repairs to a minimum and made little effort to find or to purchase spares. Before long Gilfords HX3464 and VE8761 were also dismantled and derelict. The drivers did their best to keep the survivors running, these being the Bedford (BVE668) and the remaining four Gilfords. All now had to be started by hand, for the starter motors were removed and stored as and when they failed.

The situation might have become impossible had it not been for Mr M J Gifford, who joined the company as a driver early in 1941. Mr Gifford had an engineering background and had previously worked in the road transport industry, and he was persuaded to help with the maintenance difficulties. These had now reached crisis proportions, and Mr Gifford set to work. The starter motors were repaired and put back. The missing parts of CCE568 were also found, and by the end of 1941 the Dennis was mechanically complete even if it lacked some of its former splendour.

Early in 1942, two Ministry of Transport officials visited Harston and inspected the derelict Gilfords. The officials arranged for the vehicles to be repaired and returned to service, so great was the need for transport. The parts for HX3464 were located, and the decidedly unhealthy-sounding Gilford was driven to Biggleswade where the necessary repairs were carried out. Some of the missing pieces were also restored to VE8761, and the incomplete vehicle was towed to Whitwell for the rest of the work to be done. Meanwhile CCE568 developed further engine trouble which required re-grinding and new bearings, and the Ministry Men made the necessary arrangements. Mr Gifford carefully drove the coach to Newmarket, where the problems were rectified. The Dennis also received a startling repaint in all-over dark blue, giving it the appearance of an enormous hearse.

A situation had thus been achieved which would not long before would have seemed impossible; all eight vehicles were operational, and despite the shortages and problems Mr Gifford's team managed to keep them roadworthy. The fitters still had to perform miracles, often working late into the night to provide enough runners for the following day. The Ministry officials were tolerant and understanding, although they regularly presented long lists of defects which had to be rectified in the interests of safety and reliability. Mr Gifford joined the forces in 1943, returning after hostilities ended. He later became Chief Engineer and a Director of the company, remaining with Premier until his retirement. The garage staff were joined by Frank Grice, a young evacuee who soon transferred to the Traffic Department and rose to the position of Traffic Manager after the war.

Returning to 1943, the company was still short of vehicles, and was turning away work as a result. The hire of a double-decker from London Transport was considered; this would have eliminated the need for some relief buses, but was not possible because of Premier's limited maintenance facilities. The situation gradually improved, however, and the first fleet additions were made since the outbreak of war. Coach production had ceased in 1939, and new vehicles of any kind were in very short supply. Only Bedford, Daimler and Guy were still manufacturing PSV chassis, and in September 1943 Premier managed to buy a new Bedford OWB. With its basic 'utility' body ECE879 had only the bare essentials included, but any extra vehicles were welcome. Two more Bedfords followed in 1944: ECE948 arrived in January, followed by EER242 in September. In the meantime Gilford WG1284 was destroyed by fire near Foxton in July.

Two secondhand coaches were also obtained towards the end of the war. MO8513 was a Dennis F from Windsorian Coaches, and TF1555 was a Leyland Tiger which arrived in February 1945 from Rowe, of Cudworth. The Leyland (Premier's first) was a notable machine. New to The Furness Omnibus Company in 1930, it passed in the same year to Ribble. By 1945 it had acquired a secondhand Alexander 32-seat coach body, and here was one of the main idiosyncrasies. The body often tried to go straight ahead while the chassis was turning a corner, so the cab tended to sway about, often trapping the driver's fingers between the steering wheel and the cab side. Gear-changing was also an acquired art, but TF's engine was among the best in the fleet in terms of acceleration, even if it produced rather a lot of black smoke in the process. Piloting the old Tiger was a challenge, summed up by one driver who wrote simply "Words fail me" on the defect sheet. Attempts were made to strengthen the body and, perhaps surprisingly, the vehicle survived until 1951.

This vehicle was the first Bedford to receive a non-utility body after the war ended, although it had the wartime OWB chassis. It arrived in a maroon livery, and is illustrated with a healthy load in this wartime view. It was repainted in standard livery soon afterwards, and lasted until 1959 when it was sold for scrap. *J F Parke*

This was the first of three Bedford OWB buses acquired during the war. The angular Duple bodies had 32 wooden seats which offered little comfort, and passengers sometimes slid off them on winding country lanes. The folding doors had a habit of swinging open, and this made the ride rather draughty. This post-war view at Saffron Walden was taken after upholstered seats had been fitted. *R Marshall*

New to the Furness Omnibus Company and owned for a time by Ribble, the chassis of this characterful Leyland Tiger TS1 did not appear to be very firmly attached to the secondhand Alexander coach body when the vehicle was acquired in 1945. Uniforms are much in evidence in the crowd boarding the vehicle, seen here at Drummer Street. It survived until 1951.
J F Parke

The Bedford OWBs were to have long lives, continuing in service with improved seating for many years after the war ended. They were joined in August 1945 by EER570, the first postwar Bedford to receive a non-utility body.

The improvement in the company's financial position was largely due to the appointment in July 1944 of Mr W F Matthews as a Director. Mr Matthews was a well-known local businessman who had great confidence in Premier's future, and the family connection was strengthened two years later when his son, Mr F N Matthews, also joined the firm. For many years the names of Lainson and Matthews were to play a major part in the development of Premier Travel, which had managed to survive the war and was now about to increase its operations dramatically.

THE GREAT EXPANSION
1945-1950

Premier Travel started operations by acquiring two established independents, and over the next few years discussions were held with several others. Eventually five of these operators were taken over, for this was a time of uncertainty in the industry. A Labour government had been returned in 1945, and there were now increasing fears of nationalisation. Many operators decided to get out while the going was good, and sold their businesses. Premier Travel's optimistic Directors were undaunted by the government's plans, and the company expanded considerably in the early post-war period.

The first operator to be acquired was F E Weeden, based at Chrishall on the Cambs/Herts/Essex borders. Mr Weeden began operations soon after World War One, under the 'Heydon & District' fleetname, in the neighbouring village of that name, and the fleet wore a chocolate and maroon livery. The takeover had been considered in 1936, and negotiations restarted in March 1945. The purchase of the licences, vehicles and depot was completed on 30th May, and Mr Weeden stayed on to assist the new manager at Chrishall. The takeover provided several valuable routes, including three express services. The routes were numbered as follows:

Service
6	Great Chishill - Chrishall - Saffron Walden - Clacton (summer).
7	Heydon - Chrishall - Clavering - London (Finsbury Park).
8	Cambridge - Whittlesford - RAF Duxford.
9	Great Chishill - Chrishall - Sawston - Cambridge.
10	Chrishall - Clavering - Bishop's Stortford.
11	Chrishall - Clavering - Saffron Walden.
12	Great Chishill - Chrishall - Littlebury - Saffron Walden.
13	Linton - Bartlow - Ashdon - Saffron Walden.
14	Saffron Walden - Ashdon - Radwinter - Saffron Walden (circular).

Service 7 was the first Premier route to London. It ran on Fridays only, and on 9th November 1945 it became the company's first express service to operate after the lifting of wartime restrictions on such services. Service 8 was also advertised as an express, with up to four daily journeys, some of which continued to the WAAF Headquarters at Thriplow Turn. Service 6 did not recommence until the following spring, while the bus routes ran mostly for local markets and none offered a daily service, although some ran on Sundays. A varied assortment of vehicles joined the fleet, including another Gilford (WG1273, similar to WG1284 which had been lost in the previous year), two Albions (BCE372 and CUR921), a Bedford WTB (CVE424) and another pair of utility Bedford OWB buses (EER99 and ECE794). The largest vehicle was another pre-war Dennis Lancet (CVE12).

This postwar view shows Bedford OWB EER570 at Chrishall depot after performing a journey on Service 9 from Cambridge. A comparison with the illustration on page 14 shows how Premier's standard livery improved the appearance of this vehicle. *Derek Parsons*

Seven vehicles were acquired from Weeden of Chrishall, including two additional Bedford OWB buses. This one had a Duple body and was photographed at Drummer Street in Cambridge. It survived for fifteen years with Premier Travel before ending its days as a contractor's site hut in the Mildenhall area. The other ex-Weeden OWB had a much shorter life with Premier, lasting only until 1947 when it was sold for further service. *R. Marshall*

The takeover of Weeden's also introduced Albion vehicles into an already varied fleet. This PK114 model had a Waveney 26-seat coach body, and was fitted with a Perkins diesel engine by Premier. The panels in the side windows show some of the important points on Service 5, unlike the destination blind which reveals very little! After withdrawal in 1952 this coach was presented to Cambridgeshire County Council and became a mobile road safety exhibition. *G R Mills collection*

The ex-Weeden's Dennis Lancet was similar to CCE568. It is fondly remembered for its superb riding qualities, although with its plodding 4-cylinder engine it took its time to build up speed and earned the nickname 'The Old Thumper'. Despite its lumbering progress, it gave another thirteen years faithful service and was one of the last pre-war coaches in the fleet. *M Seabrook collection*

By the end of 1945 the company's financial position was very healthy. Regular excursions to Newmarket Races started from Sawston and Saffron Walden, and a large volume of private hire was once again handled. Traffic demands still led to maintenance difficulties, especially with the pre-war vehicles. There was continued dissatisfaction with the Dennis F and the Leyland TS1, and the disposal was considered of most of the Gilfords, which were increasingly expensive to maintain. Other plans were made: the company had acquired land in Cambridge at 215-217 Newmarket Road (opposite Coldham's Lane), with the intention of building a depot and coach station when restrictions on new buildings were relaxed. This never happened, and the site was later sold.

Negotiations for the takeover of Drayton's of Barley began in November; nationalisation of bus and coach operators was not included in the King's Speech in 1945, and the Directors felt that the discussions should proceed with Draytons, as well as with other operators. If Premier Travel were nationalised, compensation would be forthcoming for the assets, however long they had been owned, and it was decided that expansion should continue. To make sure that its opposition to the government's plans did not go unheard, the company joined the Passenger Vehicle Operators Association in November 1945.

Premier published a complete timetable of all its services on the first day of 1946. With exhortations to 'support independent enterprise' this impressive publication included a route map, a list of local market days, and numerous advertisements for local businesses. As well as Services 1-14, it also, listed Service 15 (Little Walden - Saffron Walden, a section still busy 40 years later), and Service 16, which began as a single journey on weekdays from RAF Duxford to nearby Whittlesford railway station. Initially intended to serve the needs of the aerodrome, this route was soon extended at both ends to become a useful Stapleford - Sawston - Royston market day service. Other services were numbered S1, S2 and S3. Service S1 provided transport for employees of Pye's of Cambridge, reaching their Haig Road factory after a roundabout journey from Harston. The Pye (now Philips) factories, of which there were eventually several in the area, were to play a vital part in the fortunes of Premier Travel. W G Pye originally established his business to supply scientific instruments to the University, and went on to produce wireless sets (as they were then called), televisions and telecommunications equipment. Additional staff were needed for Pye's post-war expansion, and Service S1 began following urgent discussions with the Works Manager, Mr Jones. Other Pye contracts started from Oakington and Buntingford, and a network grew which eventually brought workers in from as far afield as Bury St Edmunds, Downham Market, March and Wisbech. Premier Travel always had a very close relationship with Pye, and some of the contracts still operate. Services S2 and S3 were restricted to schoolchildren, serving schools in Sawston and Royston respectively. School buses would also continue to provide regular income, although after 1946 contract services did not appear in the public timetables.

Expansion continued, and discussions took place with R F Brand of Elsworth, and A J Gill of Godmanchester. The Brand's business was not acquired (it passed to Whippet Coaches many years later), but Mr Gill's services passed to Premier Travel from March 1st, together with four rather unhealthy vehicles, in a pale blue livery. There were two small Bedford WLB buses (EW7332 and JF2725) and two more Gilfords; WG329 was another former Alexander specimen, while Premier Travel became the *ninth* owner of

The company continued to purchase secondhand Gilford coaches in the early post-war years, but few can have had as many previous owners as this one. It was new in 1933 to Strawhatter Motor Coaches of Luton, passing to London Transport in the following year. It was subsequently owned by no fewer than five other operators before passing to Gill's of Godmanchester, from whom Premier Travel acquired it in 1946. It had a Strachans body and was photographed in the snow at Drummer Street in 1947. The rear view shows the original style of lettering including the company's address and telephone number. This was later replaced by a simple 'Premier Travel' fleetname in the style of larger operators. The original Bedford WTB (BVE668) is also in evidence. *K Worland collection*

MJ2154, which had been new to Strawhatter of Luton before passing to London Transport for use on Green Line services. Gill's operated several infrequent bus services in the sparsely-populated area around their home town. The new owners hoped for a considerable increase of business in the locality; the young Frank Matthews was appointed Depot Manager at Godmanchester and promised every assistance by the Board. Four acres of land were acquired including a cottage, additional buildings were erected and ex-Weeden's Albion BCE372 became an office and rest room at the depot. The ex-Gill's services initially continued as before, running from Godmanchester and neighbouring Huntingdon to St Ives (Service 19) and St Neots (Services 17 and 20), with Service 17 continuing to Bedford. Service 18 was the most frequent and ran on four days of the week, following a circular route from Godmanchester and Huntingdon to RAF Upwood, again illustrating the presence of the armed forces in the area. These services were isolated from Premier's other bus routes, although express and contract vehicles regularly passed through the area. The buses were very busy on market days, and larger vehicles soon appeared.

In the same month as the Gill's takeover, Premier also purchased the licence for the express service of W H Thorne of Clacton. This eventually became Service 35 and consisted of a single Clacton to London journey on summer Saturdays; passengers made the outward journey by steamer, then still a popular method of reaching the east coast resorts from London. No vehicles were acquired from Mr Thorne.

Until 1939 Clacton had been served by Service 5 and by the Weeden's route from Great Chishill, now Service 6. The 1946 timetable assured hopeful travellers that Services 4, 5 and 6 would be restored in time for the holiday season. Also promised were "coach cruises", although there were warnings that "many wartime problems still confront us:- several of our staff are still in the forces, spare parts are difficult to obtain, we are still heavily engaged on special priority transport, and new luxury coaches are not yet available". The express services duly recommenced, however, and a comprehensive range of excursions was advertised, although the removal of signposts (carried out as a security measure during the war) caused problems to new drivers. Upholstered seats were fitted to the utility Bedfords to make them more suitable for long-distance work, and two more old Leyland Tigers arrived during the summer. These were AG6221, a TS1 originally with Western SMT, and GJ5124, a TS3 acquired from Mascot of Norwich but new to Eastern Counties.

This Leyland Tiger TS3 was acquired in 1946 from Votier of Norwich, although it had been new to Eastern Counties in 1930 as VF7660. It had a United 28-seat body and was one of several elderly Leylands added to stock after the war when passenger numbers were increasing and new vehicles were in short supply. It had a short life with Premier, lasting only until the end of 1948.
J F Higham

21

The first new vehicle for two years arrived during February 1947, in the shape of a Bedford OB (FER241), again with a Duple bus body. Operations also began on the 'Inter-Varsity Express' service. Initially unnumbered, this ran from Cambridge to Oxford via Royston, Hitchin, Luton and Aylesbury, although passengers for intermediate points could not be carried because of railway objections. It was operated jointly with the old-established operator R Moore, trading as Percival's Motors (Cambridge) Ltd, whose pale blue and cream coaches ran from cramped premises in King Street. In theory the joint operators worked alternately, but in practice Premier Travel provided the service more often in summer, when Mr Moore's three coaches were busy with private hire and excursion work. The Inter-Varsity Express initially ran only on Sundays, with one return journey during University terms, but it later became increasingly important as the Cambridge - Oxford railway service declined and eventually ceased. The former Undergraduate Roadways operation to Skegness was also resurrected, with Service 3 now running via St Ives and Ramsey, giving many villages a direct summer service on Saturdays and Sundays.

Meetings with other operators continued, including discussions in May with Mr H Lee regarding the possible takover of Whippet Coaches of Hilton. Had this happened it would have firmly established Premier Travel in the Huntingdon area, but nothing came of the negotiations. Shortly afterwards, however, the former Gill's services were strengthened and augmented by several new ones, as follows:

Service
21   Godmanchester - Huntingdon - Barnwell St Andrew - Oundle.
22   Abbots Ripton - RAF Upwood - St Ives.
24   Godmanchester - Huntingdon - Abbots Ripton - The Giddings - Hemington.
25   Huntingdon - Grafham - The Staughtons - Pertenhall.

Among the vehicles acquired from Drayton's of Barley in September 1947 was this Plaxton-bodied Bedford WTB, which was scrapped after ten years service. It was to be many years before Premier Travel purchased any further coaches with this make of body, although the company standardised on AEC/Plaxton coaches from 1975 onwards.
D W Parsons

The Dennis Pike acquired from Drayton's had a Duple 20-seat body and was one of only fifteen examples built. It was not the fastest of vehicles, and its door could be operated by a lever which unwary drivers sometimes confused with the handbrake. Stopping on a hill could lead to some surprise when the lever was pulled, the door opened and the coach started rolling down the slope!
J C Gillham

Premier also applied to run buses to Ramsey, but Eastern National successfully objected. The new routes served a very sparsely-populated area, and were rarely busy. September saw the start of market day Service 23 (Stapleford - Sawston - Saffron Walden) in response to public requests. In the same month came the takeover of A Drayton (t/a 'Drayton's Motor Services') of Barley, not far from Chrishall. The Drayton's business was similar in character to that of Weeden's, with local bus services and another London express. Drayton's vehicles wore a dark blue and cream livery, and eight more assorted coaches joined Premier's varied selection. There were two more Gilfords (JH4429 and WG1286), three Bedford WTBs, including one with a Plaxton body (BAJ161, BFD955 and CWD840) and another Duple-bodied Dennis Lancet (ENK387). Other noteworthy additions were a Leyland Cub with a rear entrance (the first such vehicle with Premier, registered FD9601), and a rare 20-seat Dennis Pike (DRO972), one of only fifteen built.

The services taken over (with Drayton's service numbers in brackets) were:

Service
12A (2) Chrishall - Gt Chishill - Barley - Barkway - Reed - Royston.
26 (1) Royston - Barley/Newsells - Barkway - The Pelhams - Bishop's Stortford.
27 (4) Nuthampstead - Barkway - Barley - Gt Chishill - Fowlmere - Cambridge.
28 (6) Chrishall - Gt Chishill - Barley - Barkway - London (King's Cross).
29 (5) Barley - Barkway/Royston - Reed - Therfield - Sandon - Baldock - Letchworth - Hitchin.

The London-bound Service 28 coach departed from Chrishall on Friday mornings, and soon afterwards it met the London-bound Service 7 coach travelling in the opposite direction. Service 26 was the most frequent, with a daily service. Service 12A (the only A-suffixed number ever used) also had market day journeys via Shaftenhoe End, while there were also market day buses from Sandon to Royston on Service 29. Hitchin was served on Tuesdays and Sundays, the lengthy journey taking 85 minutes. The acquisition of the Drayton routes established Premier Travel as the main operator along the Saffron Walden - Chrishall - Royston axis. The garage in Barley continued to be owned by the Drayton family, and bears their name to this day. Premier operated its new routes from Chrishall, where alterations to existing services provided daily links from Chrishall to Saffron Walden (Service 12) and to Cambridge (Service 9), with additional buses from Cambridge to Stapleford (Haverhill Road Corner) on the latter service. Various evening services were also restored, and new offices were opened in Saffron Walden and Huntingdon, which participated in the growing travel agency side of the business.

While Premier Travel grew, the politicians had been busy. The Transport Act of 1947 came into force on the first day of 1948, and the Tilling group of bus companies, (including Eastern Counties and Eastern National) became part of the new British Transport Commision, along with London Transport. Premier Travel continued along its independent way, however, and another new Bedford OB (GCE422) joined the fleet in January 1948, this time with a Mulliner bus body. Premier now had eight Bedford OWB and OB buses, five of which had been purchased new. Interestingly, they were the only single-deck buses (as opposed to coaches) which were ever bought new, although coaches regularly appeared on the bus routes. The new bus was followed in June by a Duple-bodied coach version (GER422) while a larger coach, again with a Duple body, came in the shape of the first post-war Dennis Lancet (GER217). Other new additions were two Daimler CVD6 coaches (GCE654/655). They were Premier's first Daimlers, and their arrival began a brief association with the Leeds coachbuilders Wilks & Meade. This firm had been associated with the large Wallace Arnold company since 1945, and also built the body for GER140, the first of four new Leyland Tiger PS1/1 coaches, which arrived in October.

Two of these Daimler CVD6 coaches were purchased new in 1948. They were the company's first Daimlers, and some drivers took a while to get used to the preselective gearboxes, although these were sometimes useful for moving standing passengers to the back of the coach when pulling away from stops! The Daimlers also began Premier Travel's brief association with Wilks & Meade, one of the many small manufacturers who produced bodywork in the early post-war years when new vehicles were urgently needed. The side destination blinds are clearly evident in this view. *R H G Simpson*

Other significant purchases in 1948 were three elderly Leyland Titans, the company's first double-deckers. These were necessary because of the boom then being enjoyed by bus operators, and they provided valuable extra capacity at a time when passenger numbers were rapidly increasing. The first arrived in April from Oldham Corporation (BU7601), and was a TD1 with a highbridge English Electric body. The others were a pair of all-Leyland lowbridge TD2s (DW6942/6944) from Red & White of Chepstow. These appeared in August and had fairly short careers. In March of the following year DW6942 caught fire while working on Service 9 and was almost totally destroyed (fortunately there were no injuries), while DW6944 was withdrawn just over a year later.

The Cambridge - Royston services were co-ordinated with those of Eastern Counties towards the end of the year, when it was finally agreed that Premier Travel should operate two daily journeys to Royston on Service 2, which previously ran only as far as Barrington, except on Wednesdays. The section of Service 2 via Hauxton village was covered by Service 27 and by some journeys on Service 1. Return, season and weekly tickets became inter-available between common points on Services 1, 2 and 27 and Eastern Counties Service 108. This arrangement continued for many years and provided passengers with a better service, although conductors did not appreciate the extra waybills they had to complete when accepting Eastern Counties tickets. A condition of the agreement was that Premier withdrew its application to pick up and set down in Trumpington on Service 9 (Great Chishill - Chrishall - Cambridge).

The company's first double-deckers were past their prime when they arrived in 1948. This English Electric-bodied Leyland TD1 started life with Oldham Corporation, and was photographed at Drummer Street before its original petrol engine was replaced by a diesel unit. It was notable for its clutch, or more precisely the apparent lack of one when it first arrived. On one memorable occasion four experienced drivers all failed their upgrade test because of gear-changing difficulties with the brute, although this problem was later rectified and the bus lasted for four years. A Burwell & District Daimler utility stands behind. *G R Mills collection*

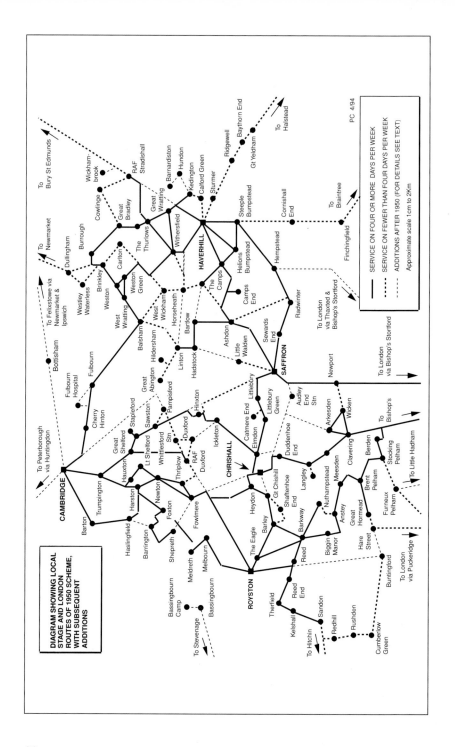

DIAGRAM SHOWING LOCAL STAGE AND LONDON ROUTES OF 1950 SCHEME, WITH SUBSEQUENT ADDITIONS

SERVICE ON FOUR OR MORE DAYS PER WEEK

SERVICE ON FEWER THAN FOUR DAYS PER WEEK

ADDITIONS AFTER 1950 (FOR DETAILS SEE TEXT)

Approximate scale 1cm to 2Km

PC 4/94

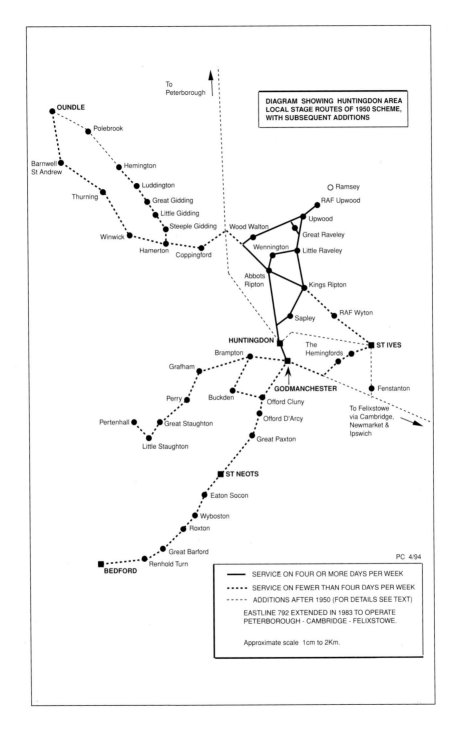

DIAGRAM SHOWING HUNTINGDON AREA
LOCAL STAGE ROUTES OF 1950 SCHEME,
WITH SUBSEQUENT ADDITIONS

To Peterborough

OUNDLE
Polebrook
Barnwell St Andrew
Hemington
Thurning
Luddington
Great Gidding
Little Gidding
Steeple Gidding
Winwick
Hamerton
Coppingford
Wood Walton
Wennington
Abbots Ripton
Sapley
Brampton
Grafham
Perry
Buckden
Pertenhall
Great Staughton
Little Staughton
Offord Cluny
Offord D'Arcy
Great Paxton

Ramsey
RAF Upwood
Upwood
Great Raveley
Little Raveley
Kings Ripton
RAF Wyton
HUNTINGDON
The Hemingfords
ST IVES
GODMANCHESTER
Fenstanton

To Felixstowe
via Cambridge,
Newmarket &
Ipswich

ST NEOTS
Eaton Socon
Wyboston
Roxton
Great Barford
Renhold Turn
BEDFORD

PC 4/94

—————— SERVICE ON FOUR OR MORE DAYS PER WEEK
▪▪▪▪▪▪ SERVICE ON FEWER THAN FOUR DAYS PER WEEK
- - - - - ADDITIONS AFTER 1950 (FOR DETAILS SEE TEXT)
EASTLINE 792 EXTENDED IN 1983 TO OPERATE
PETERBOROUGH - CAMBRIDGE - FELIXSTOWE.

Approximate scale 1cm to 2Km.

In complete contrast to the double-deckers, three more new coaches arrived early in 1949. GER141/834/835 were additional Leyland Tiger PS1/1 vehicles with Wilks & Meade bodies identical to GER140, delivered in the previous autumn. A feature of the Wilks & Meade bodied coaches was the liberal provision of destination boxes, with no fewer than four along each side in addition to those at the front and rear. The side blinds could be used to show the full extent of long routes, so that BIRMINGHAM - LEICESTER - CAMBRIDGE-CLACTON ON SEA could be proudly displayed, although this involved a lot of arm exercise for the drivers. Some coaches later had the side and rear blinds removed.

Another secondhand double-decker also arrived, in the shape of a Leyland TD4c from Plymouth Corporation (JY6739). Further double-deckers came in May with the takeover of Long's Coaches of West Wratting, latterly owned by Mr & Mrs Towse, who operated five vehicles in a bright yellow livery with black relief. Three of these joined the Premier fleet, comprising an ex-Birmingham Daimler COG5 (AOP777), and two ex-City of Oxford AEC Regents (JO8456/JO8663), all with highbridge bodies. A Leyland Lion LT7 coach (TJ9275) was also acquired, but never operated. Some of Long's routes were eventually numbered as follows:

Service
44   Gt Bradley - West Wratting - Fulbourn - Cambridge.
45   Burrough Green - West Wratting - Fulbourn - Cambridge.
48   West Wratting - Burrough Green - Gt Bradley - Haverhill.
49   Balsham - West Wratting - Horseheath - Haverhill.
50   Haverhill - Withersfield - Gt Thurlow.

Service 44 ran daily and Service 45 every weekday, and these two routes became increasingly important. The rest ran on market days, along with other services from the West Wratting area to Newmarket, Saffron Walden and Haverhill. Facilities at the West Wratting depot were fairly basic, with no mains electricity, and it closed soon afterwards. After it ceased to be an operational depot it became a graveyard for withdrawn vehicles, which were stored there prior to sale, usually for scrapping. Operation of all the ex-Long's services was transferred to the depot in Camps Road, Haverhill, which was taken over very soon afterwards with G F Burgoin's 'Grey Pullman Coaches'. The Burgoin's business was a valuable purchase, for Haverhill was about to expand, following its designation by the London County Council as an overspill town. Its size increased greatly over the next twenty years as new houses and factories were built. Foremost among the Burgoin routes was the daily Thurlow - Haverhill - Bumpsteads - Radwinter - Saffron Walden service, with an express section on to London, which also served Cowlinge and RAF Stradishall at weekends. This became Service 38. Other services were less frequent, becoming:

Service
52   Haverhill - RAF Stradishall.
53   Haverhill - Ridgewell - Gt Yeldham - Halstead.
55   Haverhill - Withersfield/Gt Wratting - Cowlinge - Bury St Edmunds.
58   Haverhill - The Bumpsteads - Cornishall End - Finchingfield - Braintree.
60   Haverhill - Kedington - Calford Green - Haverhill (Circular).

A former City of Oxford AEC Regent I, one of a pair previously operated in the yellow and black livery of Long's Coaches of West Wratting. They had highbridge bodywork, in this case by Weymann. The bus is seen leaving Drummer Street on the ex-Weeden's Service 9, which became increasingly important after Premier Travel took over. It became a daily service in 1947, with additional buses to Haverhill Road Corner in Stapleford. The two Regents survived with Premier until 1952. *A B Cross*

The former Long's services were soon transferred to Haverhill depot, and they steadily developed to become some of Premier Travel's most important routes. Highbridge double-deckers could not be operated there because of the low railway bridge next to Haverhill station, and lowbridge vehicles with their awkward side gangways and four-in-a-row seating upstairs were a feature of the area's bus routes for many years. This sparkling ex-Plymouth Leyland TD4c had a lowbridge Weymann body and was purchased in 1949. It served Premier for just over five years. *M Seabrook collection*

As with Long's, there were other market-day routes into Haverhill and Saffron Walden, and together with the remaining ex-Long's services they were combined to form several new routes in the great reorganisation which took place during the following summer. Burgoin's vehicles wore a grey and green livery, and most were Bedfords, with characteristic West Suffolk registrations. There were two WTBs, one WLB, five OB coaches (one with a Thurgood body) and an OB bus (GV9861), together with a Gilford (GV2405 - the last to be purchased), a Leyland Cub with a Burlingham body (CS4326) and a Willowbrook-bodied AEC Regal III (BGV401), Premier's first AEC coach. The OBs and the Regal had long and useful lives, lasting until the early 1960s. Another Cub (GV2605) and a Reo (GV406) were also acquired, but not operated. Premier made plans for a major rebuilding of Haverhill depot, to include a coach station and cafe, but only a booking office was ever provided, and the town did not have a bus station until 1977.

The 1949 takeovers took Premier's service numbers up to 60, but in the meantime several new express services had been introduced during the summer. These were:

Service
34   Bedford - Gt Barford - Boston - Wainfleet - Skegness.
36   Ramsey - Huntingdon - Godmanchester - Cottenham - Histon - Norwich - Gt Yarmouth.
37   Berden - Clavering - Saffron Walden - Linton - Haverhill - RAF Stradishall - Lowestoft - Gt Yarmouth.

Operations were on Saturdays, from the end of May to the end of September. The other new routes were leave services from local RAF stations. Direct links were provided from RAF Upwood to King's Cross (Service 30) and to Leicester, Coventry and Birmingham (Service 31). Additional journeys from RAF Stradishall to King's Cross were provided by Service 32, although the Service 38 journeys between these points continued. Departure from the aerodromes was at midday on Fridays and Saturdays, returning late on Sunday evenings, with extra journeys as required. A more humble operation was Service 33, a solitary journey from Cambridge railway station to RAF Oakington at 0100 on Mondays only, which always carried a healthy load. All the leave services were restricted to personnel from the bases concerned. RAF Duxford continued to be served by ex-Weeden's Service 8, advertised as an express, although no advance booking was necessary. An application was made in the summer of 1947 to increase this service between Whittlesford (the only intermediate stop) and Cambridge, but this was refused. The presence of the RAF provided business for Premier Travel for many years, the services continuing to run until the 1960s, when the aerodromes closed.

By the end of 1949 the takeovers were complete. In just over four years the company had greatly increased its size and its area of operation. Premier Travel's bus services now operated in seven counties (Cambridgeshire, West Suffolk, Essex, Hertfordshire, Huntingdonshire, Northamptonshire and Bedfordshire). Excursions, tours, private hires and contracts were also operated, and the express network was still growing. New facilities were provided on the London services just before Christmas, with Service 7 now starting from Ickleton, and Service 28 from Fowlmere, and further exciting developments were imminent. Premier Travel had become an established part of the bus and coach scene in the Cambridge area.

One of a number of small Bedfords in Burgoin's 'Grey Pullman' fleet, this WLB had a Bush & Twiddy 20-seat body and was already 15 years old when taken over. Its original owner is unknown, but it operated for neighbouring Burwell & District before Burgoin's purchased it in 1937. Photographed at Haverhill depot, it was withdrawn by Premier at the end of 1951. *J F Higham*

Another former Burgoin Bedford was this WTB with a Duple 26-seat body. Photographed at Oxford during the 1950s, it looks rather dated alongside the underfloor-engined coach beside it, although Premier did not purchase any modern coaches until 1959, two years after this coach had been withdrawn. *R H G Simpson*

One of the oldest coaches from the Burgoin fleet was this forward-control Leyland Cub. Dating from 1935, it had a Burlingham body and was photographed at Godmanchester depot. A similar vehicle (but with a rear entrance) was acquired from Drayton's two years earlier. *J C Gillham*

The largest of the ex-Burgoin vehicles was this Willowbrook-bodied AEC Regal III seen here at Haverhill depot. It was the first AEC coach in the fleet and it lasted until 1963. Premier became a very enthusiastic AEC user, and purchased no other make of chassis from 1968 until AEC ceased production. Such standardisation was not possible in the early post-war years, when operators had to do the best they could with the vehicles available, and the Regal remained the only such vehicle in the fleet. *G R Mills*

Burgoin's daily Thurlow-Haverhill-Saffron Walden route included an express section on to London. It also served RAF Stradishall, and as Service 38 it became Premier's fourth London service. Burgoin's newest vehicles were five Bedford OB coaches, and this one was photographed preparing to leave Saffron Walden on its two-hour journey to the capital. *R Marshall*

At the start of 1950 three more new coaches were delivered, all with Duple bodies, these being another Bedford OB (HVE242) and two more Dennis Lancets (HVE36 and HVE707, of which HVE36 had been ordered by Drayton's before the takeover). Three more double-deckers also joined the fleet, but unlike those purchased previously they were new, and were among the company's most interesting vehicles. The first was HVE401, which arrived in April, with HVE402/403 following in June and July. Their Daimler CVD6 chassis had originally been ordered by Dundee Corporation, and they received bodywork by Wilks & Meade, the same chassis/body combination as GCE654/655, delivered two years earlier. Believed to be the only double-deckers ever bodied by Wilks & Meade, the new arrivals were unusual in several ways. They had full fronts, concealed radiators and platform doors, features which were uncommon in 1950, when most double-deckers had half cabs and open platforms. Internally there were 53 coach seats and the added luxury of heaters, and the ride was excellent. This was partly due to the bodywork, which was very heavy, so heavy in fact that the front suspension had to be modified. There were other problems. Not all drivers liked the full-width cabs, which became rather hot in summer, and fumes from the engines sometimes made life uncomfortable. The bodywork later caused far more serious difficulties, but when they arrived the Daimlers attracted a great deal of attention. HVE401 was officially named 'County of Cambridge' by the Chairman of Cambridgeshire County Council, while HVE402/403 (without ceremony) became 'County of West Suffolk' and 'County of Essex' respectively.

The Wilks & Meade-bodied Daimler CVD6 double-deckers were probably the most famous vehicles owned. Their styling was very much in keeping with contemporary coach practice, the curved and pointed mouldings giving them a distinctly 'streamlined' look. All three received names, and 'County of Cambridge' stands proudly outside the University Arms Hotel in Cambridge, the scene of its naming ceremony on April 17th 1950. The panels above the lower deck windows read 'Birmingham-Leicester-Cambridge-Clacton', giving a clue to the intended use of these coaches, although they were never allowed to operate on Service 5. *Courtesy A J Weir*

The 'County' Daimlers also appeared on private hire duties. Seen at Harlow, the rear view of 'County of Essex' shows the folding platform doors and the distinctive three-window layout incorporating the emergency exit. The combination of high-backed seats, small windows and low ceilings made these coaches rather dark downstairs, although there were skylights on the upper deck to brighten things up. The rear destination blinds were removed when the bodies were completely rebuilt during the 1950s. *J C Gillham*

The company intended to operate the double-deck coaches on express services, and planned to purchase more if the 'County' class vehicles were successful, even placing an order for six Leyland PD2 chassis. Unfortunately, the licensing authorities were less enthusiastic, and the use of the Daimlers was restricted. They were never allowed to run on Services 4 or 5, and were initially confined to routes of up to 60 miles in length. They appeared regularly on the London services, first on Service 32 from RAF Stradishall, and afterwards on Service 38. They were also used on private hire work, but in view of licensing difficulties the Leyland order was changed, with two PD2s and four Royal Tigers now expected late in 1951.

After such rapid expansion the next few years were seen as a time for consolidation and for building up traffic. At that time many of the bus services ran only once or twice a week, working to long-familiar timings established by the acquired operators. In June 1950, however, an attempt was made to increase the scope of the bus services, the intention being to operate a network of regular-frequency routes. Existing services were reorganised and linked, frequencies were increased and more new services started. An example was the linking of Services 12, 12A and 29 to provide the marathon Service 12 (Saffron Walden - Hitchin), with additional buses as far as Royston on new Service 39. It was all very complicated, and can be summarised as follows:

An interior view of the upper deck of HVE401 ('County of Cambridge'), showing the coach-style lighting and interior trim. The use of high-backed seats restricted passenger vision even more than usual in a lowbridge body, but the skylights in the roof were a welcome feature. The seats were upholstered in a mainly green moquette, and were retained after the vehicles were demoted to bus services. Access to the rear emergency window would not have been very easy! *Courtesy A J Weir*

Service

12   Saffron Walden - Littlebury - Catmere End (Wed) - Littlebury Green - Elmdon - Chrishall - Heydon - Gt Chishill - Shaftenhoe End (Tue/Wed/Sat) - Barley - Royston.
Extended Tue/Sun to Barkway (Tue) - Reed - Therfield - Kelshall - Sandon - Wallington - Baldock - Letchworth - Hitchin. Additional buses Wed/Sat Sandon - Royston.

39   Saffron Walden - Littlebury - Littlebury Green - Elmdon - Chrishall - Heydon - Gt Chishill - Barley - Barkway - Reed - Royston.

The occasional journeys from Sandon, via Shaftenhoe End and via Catmere End catered for market-day traffic, although the latter village initially had no service into nearby Saffron Walden on market day (Tuesday). Service 39 normally ran from Chrishall to Royston, the Saffron Walden section operating only on Mondays and Fridays, when neither town had a market! Some sections of these routes had daily buses, however, as did Services 1, 2, 8, 9, 26, 38 and 44. Alterations to the former Long and Burgoin routes produced new Services 46/51 (Saffron Walden - Linton/West Wickham - Newmarket), 42 (Haverhill - Bumpsteads Circular), 56 (Haverhill - Newmarket), 57 (Haverhill - Camps End - Saffron Walden), and a short-lived 47 (Balsham - Horseheath - Haverhill).

Chrishall depot became a major interchange point, with connecting facilities on Services 9, 10 and 12 (although some connections on Services 9 and 10 had previously been shown in timetables). Sometimes it was possible to stay on the same bus and such timings were later advertised, although no through fares existed, and passengers had to re-book after the bus had changed its service number and left Chrishall! Timetables were also arranged to give connections at other places, such as Barkway, Barley, Royston and Saffron Walden. The whole scheme was presented in an impressive 80-page booklet, which became known in Premier folklore as 'The Windmill Timetable' because of the design on the cover, which also featured a photograph of a new Dennis Lancet. There was also a route map, together with a full-page view of HVE401 to show off the latest idea in coach travel. All the express routes were detailed, including a new Service 29 (Kedington - Haverhill - Ashdon - Saffron Walden - London).

It was a brave scheme which proved to be over-ambitious and not entirely successful, although it maximised vehicle use and eliminated a lot of light mileage. Unfortunately the travelling public were reluctant to change their habits, and passenger numbers did not increase enough to bring in the anticipated profits. A notable example concerned Service 41 (Therfield -

Buntingford). On the first day Leyland Tiger AG6221, crewed by Messrs Pennell and Bray, performed two round trips without selling one ticket, although they did give a Smith's conductress a lift into town! This was an extreme example of a lack of traffic, but cuts quickly followed. Despite its initial promise the scheme proved to be expensive to operate, having been introduced at a time when the company could not really afford such a venture. The Directors later agreed that it offered "too much too late", and it also had to be admitted that it went on for too long, at a time when there were no council subsidies for unprofitable services.

Although bus loadings did not improve dramatically, the express services became increasingly busy. Paid holidays were now common, and holidaymakers wanted to get to the seaside. Premier served Skegness, Great Yarmouth and, most importantly, Clacton-on-Sea. New Dennis Lancet HVE36 toured the Midlands in 1950, promoting Clacton as a resort and Service 5 as the best way to get there. Enormous loads were carried and numerous relief coaches were needed, many hired at short notice. No fewer than 55 other operators hired vehicles to Premier Travel during the summer of 1949, and in the summer of 1950 over 4000 passengers travelled on Service 5 on Saturdays. An Inclusive Holiday scheme was introduced, combining coach travel with pre-booked hotel accommodation in Clacton, or Walton-on-the-Naze. The scheme operated for the next three seasons.

Premier benefited greatly from its special relationship with the mighty Midland Red company. As well as providing booking facilities throughout its operating area, Midland Red allowed the blue coaches to use Digbeth Coach Station in Birmingham, and the service also called at Pool Meadow in Coventry. The more modest facilities in Leicester consisted of a roadside stop in Red Cross Street, but this was fairly close to the Midland Red's Southgate Street premises. In Cambridge, however, Service 5 still avoided Drummer Street, calling instead at the Lensfield Road stop, inherited from Empire's Best. A booking agent was based nearby, one of many throughout the company's operating area and beyond. Some were coach operators, among them Midland Red, United Counties, Grey-Green and Birch Brothers. Others ran their agencies from shops, pubs, cafes, garages or even their own homes. All played a vital part in the build-up of the express services, which were so important to Premier's survival.

It had been a notable year, and on summer Saturdays Mr Lainson's dream of a network of coaches had become a reality. The new vehicles saw off several veterans, notably the last of the stately Gilfords, GV2405 and WG329. Further expansion and modernisation was contemplated, and discussions took place in November regarding a possible takeover of Wiffen's Coaches of Finchingfield. Replacement of the Bell Punch ticket system was also considered; Ultimate and Insert Setright machines were demonstrated, of which the latter seemed better suited to Premier's needs.

All was not well, however, and clouds were gathering. The rapid expansion on borrowed funds had left Premier Travel in a financial position which was far from secure, not helped by the introduction in the April budget of a tax on diesel fuel of 9d (3.5pence) per gallon. This staggering blow increased the annual fuel bill by £6000. Repeated representations to the Chancellor were made by the industry, but to no avail. The combined effects of the fuel tax, together with the increased costs of spares, tyres and wages led to a fares increase, but the company still made a loss, and hard times lay ahead.

CHAPTER FOUR

MORE GROWTH IN DIFFICULT TIMES
1951-1955

The next few years were far from easy. The vehicle intake slowed down considerably and there were staff reductions. Loadings failed to improve on several bus routes, with some rural sections already losing money. The Directors realised that these services fulfilled a vital and necessary function for the rural communities in the area, but the company could not continue to operate so many loss-making routes indefinitely. Service cuts required the approval of the Traffic Commissioners, however, and this was not always forthcoming. On the other hand several routes were extended and further expansion was planned despite the difficulties. Applications were made in 1951 for new express services from Cambridge to Blackpool and from Cambridge to Torquay, and for the diversion of Service 34 (Bedford - Skegness) via Rushden, but all were unsuccessful. Contract traffic increased steadily, however, and the company gained fourteen of the sixteen school contracts tendered for. Further takeovers were also considered; discussions took place with Honeywood of Stansted, and Towler of Emneth, and again with Mr Lee of Whippet Coaches, but none could be followed up because of a lack of capital. Meanwhile, Leyland Motors required a definite order for the new vehicles, or a cancellation. Premier's experience with double-deck coaches had not been successful and the order was again changed; six Royal Tiger chassis were now ordered for delivery at the end of 1952, probably to the newly-authorised width of 8 feet.

As well as the licensing difficulties with the 'County' Daimlers, the Wilks & Meade bodies were giving cause for alarm, the problem lying with the timber framing. It was rumoured that there was "a tree in each body", but because of post-war shortages, unseasoned, kiln-dried timber had been used, and this had already acquired the physical properties of balsa-wood. Pressing one's finger against the exposed parts of the frame could have alarming consequences! The single-deck coaches were similarly affected, and the only solution was to strip the bodies completely and rebuild them with new frames, made of seasoned ash. Premier was fortunate in having a very skilled body-builder on its staff, but the whole experience was a costly one which did nothing to help the company's finances. The original cost of £2370 per body had been substantially increased by Wilks & Meade and Premier delayed making the final payment, especially after the structural problems became evident. It was at about this time that Wilks & Meade ceased to build new bodywork, and were now busy renovating older coaches in the Wallace Arnold fleet. The company later became involved with commercial vehicles and accident repairs.

A large number of adjustments were made to the bus network in 1951, and two services were withdrawn. Most of Service 47 (Balsham - Haverhill) was absorbed by Service 49, although the Balsham - West Wratting section was discontinued. Service 40 (Hitchin - Clothall Bury - Cumberlow Green) also disappeared, with the Service 12 Hitchin journey diverted via Cumberlow Green on Tuesdays to compensate. The Sandon - Royston journeys on Service 12 passed to H V Richmond of Barley, but continued to appear in the Premier timetable. Service 41 (Therfield - Buntingford) was renumbered 47 and became a summer-only operation after 1952. Several routes lost their Sunday buses, with Service 27 withdrawn on that day during January and February. This service had been extended in November 1950 to start from Little Hadham, where a vehicle and driver were outstationed, and where connections were available with London Transport routes 350/350A to Hertford and Bishop's Stortford. Service 39 lost its Saffron Walden to Chrishall section and was renumbered 43, and together with Service 12 it continued to provide regular Chrishall - Royston buses.

All was not gloomy, however, and there were several expansions. Most notable was Service 40, a new summer express from Bedford, Huntingdon and Ramsey to Hunstanton. Direct services to London were now offered from Albury (Service 7), Barnardiston, Hundon and Shudy Camps (Service 29). Among several bus routes extended and increased were Services 44/45 (both now Great Wratting - Cambridge), while Service 9 was diverted via Pampisford. A new Service 41 (Cornish Hall End - Haverhill) appeared as a short-lived 'picture bus' on Saturday evenings, and, unusually, only return fares were available. The formerly unnumbered Inter-Varsity Express became Service 39.

A full excursion programme was also advertised in 1951, with weekly seaside trips to Clacton, Walton, Great Yarmouth, Southend and Skegness. Sporting events at Ascot, Doncaster and Newmarket (racing), Luton (football) and Silverstone (motor-racing) were also included, while for 3 shillings (15 pence) it was possible to enjoy a Circular Tour on Sunday afternoons and evenings, involving "...a pleasant drive of about 40 minutes". There were longer tours to such places as Kent, Norfolk and Stratford-upon-Avon, with special rates for those who spent their annual holiday trying out a different destination each day. "It's better by road, and best by Premier Travel" urged the publicity as the blue coaches departed in all directions, the drivers immaculate in their white summer uniforms.

Only one vehicle joined the fleet in 1951, this being another all-Leyland double-decker from Plymouth Corporation (JY3642). Modernisation of a different kind came when the traditional Bell Punches were at last replaced. Having rejected Ultimates, the company had considered Speed Setright machines (which were then being introduced by Eastern Counties), before finally deciding in favour of Insert Setrights. The new machines made the conductors' work a lot easier: the large, multi-coloured ticket racks were replaced by smaller ones containing only half-a-dozen or so types of ticket, as the Setrights printed the fare and registered the cash taken. Higher fares no longer necessitated several tickets per passenger.

While Premier Travel had been expanding, the government had made further nationalisation plans, including the setting-up of Area Transport Boards. There is no doubt that in the event of nationalisation ample compensation would have been forthcoming for Premier Travel's large network, but the Conservatives returned to power in 1951 and put an end to the proposals. No de-nationalisation took place and the structure of the industry remained unchanged, although there was some reorganisation of the BTC companies. The surviving independents no longer faced the possibility of being nationalised, but Premier now had other problems as debts continued to mount. The sale of the bus services was considered (not for the last time) and another fares increase was applied for, but refused. The figures for 1951 still showed a loss, but not such a large one as in the previous year.

Developments continued slowly in 1952. Service 44 was further extended, with a journey into Cambridge from RAF Stradishall on Saturday afternoons and return facilities late on Saturdays and Sundays. More leave services were started, with RAF personnel now able to travel direct to Coventry and Birmingham from Stradishall on Service 61 and from Duxford on Service 62. Premier Travel reached Manchester on a regular basis with Service 64 from Stradishall, also serving Leicester, Derby and Leek. Service 63 was shorter, consisting of a single journey from Duxford to Peterborough on Friday afternoons, the airmen having to find their own way back. The licence was also purchased from Nicholls of Clare for their RAF Stradishall - London service. Nicholls were then seeking to sell their entire business, but although Premier Travel expressed an interest control of the firm passed to Burton Coaches of Haverhill. Premier's leave services from RAF Stradishall continued to operate in conjunction with Nicholls, however.

The express network continued to expand. London Service 28 was extended to start from Newton, and more new summer services were introduced:

Service
65   Ramsey - Huntingdon - St Ives - Histon - Southend.
66   Newton - Saffron Walden - Haverhill - Felixstowe.
67   Birmingham - Coventry - Northampton - Dovercourt - Harwich.

The licence for Service 67 was acquired (for £220) from Allenways of Birmingham. It had started in 1937 despite Premier Travel's objections. The timetable noted that it provided "...convenient connections for continental steamers and motor-boat services to Felixstowe and Shotley", as well as serving the Warners' Holiday Camp at Dovercourt. Boat connections were given for other services where relevant, and all the company's timetables gave detailed information of connecting bus services, with times, fares, operators and service numbers all clearly shown. Useful rail connections were also included where relevant. The company went to a great deal of trouble to publicise its services and few people can have been unaware of this energetic approach, which was rewarded by a loyal following of satisfied, regular travellers. The continuing success of the express services led to the opening of Premier's own small booking office at Drummer Street in Cambridge in 1952, which took some of the pressure away from the overcrowded Market Hill premises. There were still disappointments, however, with unsuccessful applications for services from Birmingham to Southend, Birmingham to Felixstowe, Nottingham to Clacton and (again) Cambridge to Torquay.

The only coach added in 1952 arrived in January. It was an old Dennis Lancet from Salopia Saloon Coaches of Whitchurch, registered ANT471 and always referred to as 'The Ant'. Shortly afterwards, Leyland announced a price increase of £251 per Royal Tiger chassis, which was unacceptable and the order was finally cancelled. The company continued to rely on secondhand vehicles, and two more double-deckers were acquired. A lowbridge Daimler CWG5 from Haslingden Corporation (FTD195) appeared in May, followed in October by CVP138, a former Birmingham Corporation AEC Regent, latterly with Harvey's Coaches of Cottenham. This had previously been hired to Premier and was in very good order, although its non-standard gearbox led to some difficulties. The Regent joined the fleet towards the end of another hard year, when the fuel tax had continued to make life difficult, although a fares increase was granted.

Above The vehicle intake slowed down considerably in the early 1950s, although services continued to be extended, contract traffic was built up and full excursion programmes were offered. No more new vehicles were purchased for nine years, and the only coach to arrive in 1952 was this elderly Dennis from Salopia of Whitchurch. It was similar to the other pre-war Lancets, although the body (also by Dennis) proved to be less satisfactory than the Duple products.

Centre New to Birmingham Corporation in 1937, this AEC Regent I had that operator's characteristic style of bodywork, built in this case by Metro-Cammell. It was acquired by Premier in 1952 after service with Harvey of Cottenham, having previously operated on hire. By the time it was photographed at New Square in Cambridge it had become rather battered and had lost one of its headlamps, although it lasted for five years before withdrawal. The side indicator blind is a notable feature.

Left Seen here leaving Drummer Street, this Daimler CWG5 utility had a Brush lowbridge body and came from Haslingden Corporation in 1952. Older drivers remember it for the extreme effort needed to make any impression on its accelerator pedal, and it was one of several assorted double-deckers obtained for stage and contract work. The variety of chassis types made the engineers' job difficult, and this led to the decision to buy vehicles in batches.
All photos M Seabrook collection

Despite the problems the Pye contracts had seen a steady build-up, with some now worked by double-deckers. Many workers were brought in from the area to the north and east of Cambridge, and although the services were restricted to Pye employees they provided the sight of Premier Travel operating in what was largely an Eastern Counties stronghold. The afternoon departure from Haig Road was an impressive spectacle, as vehicles headed for distant towns and remote Fenland villages where they were parked overnight near to the homes of their regular drivers. These contracts provided regular income all year round when most of the express services were seasonal.

There was one more change to the local bus scene during 1952 when, as part of the BTC's reorganisation, the Midland area of Eastern National was transferred to United Counties. There was competition between United Counties and Premier Travel on services into Cambridge and also in Huntingdon, and early in 1953 discussions took place regarding the sale of Premier's Huntingdon area services to the larger operator, although nothing came of the proposals.

In January 1953 another double-decker arrived. BGA60 was a Weymann-bodied Leyland TD5 from Glasgow Corporation. It was joined in July by HWA277 (known as 'Hiawatha'), a Leyland TD7 with Northern Coachbuilders body, from Sheffield Corporation. The double-deckers were providing useful extra capacity, but the fleet now contained many different makes and types of vehicle and obtaining parts was difficult. The Directors accordingly decided that in future they would buy up to ten similar secondhand vehicles at a time, including one or two for spares.

The aerodromes continued to provide work, and two more leave services were started. Service 68 (RAF Stradishall - Doncaster - Leeds) ran jointly with Nicholls, and was extended soon afterwards to Darlington, Durham and Newcastle. Eastern Counties also applied for an RAF Stradishall - Leeds service, but this was turned down following objections by Premier Travel, as was an earlier Eastern Counties application for an RAF Stradishall - RAF Bassingbourn - Leicester - Manchester service. Premier's other new service was Service 69 (RAF Upwood - Nottingham - Derby - Manchester). No more leave services were introduced, although plans were made for a service from Stradishall to Cardiff. London Service 7 was extended to start from Sawston, and another new summer express was introduced, this being Service 70 direct from Leicester to Felixstowe. To further strengthen its position in the Midlands, Premier considered opening its own travel offices in Birmingham and Leicester, but these never materialised and the existing arrangements with Midland Red and other local agents continued. Improvements were also carried out at Harston depot, where all major engineering work was still done. With no new fleet additions the engineers were kept fully occupied, and many vehicles had their engines replaced or completely reconditioned.

As 1953 ended the company could look back on another year of expansion, although the East Coast floods and a poor summer led to a reduction in revenue on the express services. By the end of the year several old vehicles had departed, including Bedford BVE668, the company's first new vehicle. Most of the remaining old double-deckers also went, including BU7601 and the ex-Long's Regents. The first large batch of double-deckers now started to arrive, these being pre-war AEC Regents from London Transport's STL-class. One of the first was a former Country Area specimen (BLH887) with a forward entrance. "Never seen anything like it!" said one exasperated conductor, and

The half-cab coaches delivered in the immediate postwar period continued to perform front-line duties throughout the 1950s. The classic lines of this Wilks & Meade-bodied Leyland Tiger are well shown in this July 1953 view at Finchingfield, Essex. The immaculate vehicle has retained its profusion of destination boxes, while decorations for the Coronation are much in evidence. *J C Gillham*

Formerly STL1040 in the London Transport Country Area fleet, this was the only one of Premier's STLs to have a forward entrance. This was not a popular feature, although the fitting of platform doors solved the problem of dust and mud entering the lower saloon. Photographed with several tired servicemen on board, the bus displays its unusual layout. It lasted for less than three years, and there were few regrets when it was sold for scrap in April 1956. *J C Gillham*

this novel feature was far from popular to begin with. Many of Premier's routes ran along narrow country roads, and drivers had to take their charges to the very edge in order to pass other vehicles. A lot of dust blew into the STL's open doorway, and in wet weather the dust turned to mud, with predictable effects on conductors and passengers. A folding door solved this problem, but nothing could be done about the unpleasant smell peculiar to this bus. Despite concerted efforts with disinfectant, the odour was never eliminated and its source remained an unsolved mystery. Another feature of BLH887 was its slipping transmission. The other STLs all had normal rear entrances and were relatively trouble-free. Three had special bodies for working through the Blackwall and Rotherhithe Tunnels (DLU225/227/242, of which 227 was a particularly lively performer). Most arrived at intervals over the next year, the last (DGX195) appearing in 1955. Five Daimler CWA6 utilities, with AEC engines, also arrived. Two from Mansfield District (GNN664/665) and one from Glasgow Corporation (DGG916) had highbridge bodies, while a lowbridge-bodied pair came from Huddersfield Corporation (CCX651/662). To further simplify the engineering situation it was decided to place all the AECs at Chrishall, all the Leylands at Harston and most of the Daimlers at Haverhill, although the highbridge Daimlers went to Chrishall, and one Leyland to Godmanchester. A "one driver/one vehicle" policy encouraged drivers to care for their vehicles, and this continued successfully for many years. The company was still keen to update its coach fleet and towards the end of 1954 the Blackpool coachbuilder H V Burlingham offered to supply the body for a new AEC coach at the highly competitive price of £4550. This was impossible in 1955, although the AEC/Burlingham combination later became standard for the company's coaches.

The nine STLs had three different styles of bodywork, as shown in this view at New Square car park in Cambridge. DLU242 on the left was one of three built with special bodies for working the Blackwall and Rotherhithe Tunnel routes. In the centre stands BLH887, the solitary forward-entrance example purchased by Premier, by now with platform doors. DGX285 on the right had standard bodywork. The roof-mounted route number boxes on these buses were never used by Premier Travel, and they became rather battered because of overhanging trees. *M Seabrook collection*

Five utility Daimler CWA6 buses joined the fleet in 1955, including two lowbridge ones from Huddersfield Corporation. CCX662 had a Brush body and was the last in the fleet, surviving until 1960 at Haverhill depot. It is shown in Drummer Street in its last year in service alongside another Haverhill bus, former West Yorkshire Bristol K5G BWY979. The Bristol shows the very primitive blinds fitted to some of these buses when they first arrived.
M Seabrook collection

Extra stops were introduced on two summer services. Service 37 (Berden - Great Yarmouth) called additionally at Diss, Harleston, Bungay and Beccles, while the ex-Allenways Service 67 (Birmingham - Dovercourt) served Baldock, Buntingford, Bishop's Stortford, Dunmow, Braintree, Colchester and Clacton. An application to extend Service 5 to Walsall and Lichfield was turned down, as were proposals for Mansfield - Clacton and (again) Nottingham - Clacton services, the latter licence being granted to Trent and Barton. Premier also unsuccessfully opposed an application by Harper Brothers, of Heath Hayes, for a Cannock - Clacton service. The summer services were flourishing, but one small part of the network disappeared when the single journey on Service 63 (RAF Duxford - Peterborough) was withdrawn. It had the dubious distinction of being the first express service to be withdrawn permanently, although few outside the RAF can have noticed its demise. Express Service 8 (RAF Duxford - Cambridge) was also declining, and by 1955 it had almost ceased to exist except on Saturdays.

On the buses, Service 21 (Godmanchester - Barnwell St Andrew - Oundle) absorbed Service 24 which ran between the same two towns via Hemington. Both routes were very lightly-used, but in contrast Services 44/45 became increasingly busy. Both now reached Kedington, with a midweek bus into Cambridge from RAF Stradishall. Buses also served West Wickham village, having previously called only at the remote crossroads some distance away, and the build-up of traffic on Services 44/45 can be judged from the number of journeys into Cambridge. In 1949 Long's offered six Saturday buses, but the 1955 timetable showed two journeys on that day from RAF Stradishall with others from Kedington (1), Great Wratting (2), Great Bradley (2), Withersfield (1), West Wickham (1) and Fulbourn (8). All the short journeys at the Cambridge end had been introduced since Premier Travel took over.

The financial situation had become more secure, and Premier Travel's fortunes at last took a turn for the better. The expansion of services, the determination of the Directors and the loyalty of the staff turned a loss of £3069 in 1954 into a profit of £169 in 1955! The delighted Directors invited all the staff to a formal dinner, and this became an annual event. The hard work of five difficult years was now rewarded; this was the beginning of a steady improvement.

OUT OF THE WOOD
1956-1959

After the difficult years of the early 1950s, the second half of the decade saw Premier Travel become increasingly successful. Although there were further rural cuts, several new express services were introduced, and the engineering situation also improved.

Much of Premier Travel's success came from its travel agencies. The company had been agents for several travel organisations for many years, handling bookings for "steamships and airways", as the 1950 timetable stated. It was later realised that agency work for continental tour operators would bring in additional income. The bus offices accordingly became travel agencies, and a 7ft by 5ft kiosk in the entrance to the Market Hill office became Premier's first purpose-built agency. From these small beginnings grew a flourishing business, and the offices were soon handling bookings for several well-established companies, Wallace Arnold being among the first. A new agency opened in Royston in 1958, while the other offices were replaced by better, larger premises. Eventually there were travel agencies throughout the region, offering the full range of services. Their activities are outside the scope of this book, but they played an invaluable role in the growth of the Premier Travel group of companies. Premier Travel Agency Ltd became a wholly-owned subsidiary of Premier Travel in January 1964, with Mrs M M E Lainson as Managing Director.

Returning to 1956, a 'County' Daimler and a Bedford OB were entered in the British Coach Rally at Brighton. Driver Pennell of Harston depot, with BGV719, was voted Coach Driver of the Year, giving the company prestige as well as valuable publicity. Another notable trip was made in December, when Dennis Lancet HVE36 went to Vienna as part of a United Nations convoy following the invasion of Hungary. It was the first time a Premier Travel coach had been abroad, and the 3000-mile round trip was made without any mechanical problems. New Service 71 was introduced; this was another summer service to Clacton, this time from Worcester, Stratford-on-Avon, Banbury and Buckingham. A Lichfield - Clacton application was again refused, but some of the restrictions on Service 39 (Cambridge - Oxford) were lifted. Service 4 was extended from Great Yarmouth to Hemsby.

No fleet additions were made in 1956, but a modified bus livery was introduced, with cream in place of dark blue. The new scheme was applied to all subsequent buses, including the one-man saloons purchased during the 1960s. One-man buses could have reduced operating costs in 1956, although this method of working was still relatively uncommon, and in any case Premier had few suitable vehicles. Even so, it had become clear that some routes would never pay their way, and international events were now taking place which played their part in reducing unprofitable mileage. The movement of troops into the Suez Canal Zone in October was expected to safeguard oil supplies to the West. In practice it had the opposite effect; there were severe cuts in the amount of oil reaching the UK, and from 17th December, fuel rationing was introduced. Bus and coach operators were not exempt, and were required to cut their consumption. Service reductions were made from January 5th 1957,

Driver Pennell of Harston depot proudly shows the Coach Driver of the Year trophy after his success in the 1956 British Coach Rally at Brighton. Alongside stands Driver Bradman of Haverhill, who came Second in his class. Both vehicles are in immaculate condition in this official view, with stately Cambridge University buildings in the background. *Courtesy A J Weir*

This former Mansfield District Daimler CWA6 utility shows one variation of the modified bus livery introduced in 1956. Double-deckers had always been painted in the same two shades of blue as the coaches, but cream now started to replace the darker blue. Other vehicles had their roofs painted cream and the new scheme was applied to all subsequent buses including the one-man saloons purchased during the 1960s. The coach livery remained unchanged. The bus is seen at Drummer Street on Service 9. *J C Gillham*

with all of Service 23 suspended, along with sections of Services 11, 13 and 29. Journeys were cut on most other services, and warnings were given that the summer-only services (21, 22, 47 and 51) would not operate unless the situation improved. Fewer relief coaches seemed likely on the summer express services, and passengers were urged to book as early as possible. To encourage this, fares were held at 1956 levels, although in the event the services were unaffected. Rationing of diesel fuel lasted until 1st April, although petrol rationing continued until 14th May. Fuel prices increased, and operators were allowed to increase fares without the usual application to the Traffic Commissioners. And as fares went up, loadings increased because of the fuel shortage. The crisis also gave operators the opportunity to cut unprofitable mileage, and Premier withdrew Services 46 (Saffron Walden - Linton - Newmarket, Tuesdays), 47 (Therfield - Buntingford, summer Mondays) and 51 (Saffron Walden - West Wickham - Newmarket, summer Tuesdays). Other services continued to be amalgamated, or reduced. Service 23 (now Sawston - Saffron Walden) became summer only, while the Chrishall - Langley section of Service 11 was not restored immediately, although the route was later extended back as far as Duddenhoe End. The fuel situation led to a reduced British Coach Rally with no road section, held in Battersea Park. Driver Pennell was placed First in his class, again with Bedford OB BGV719.

A new summer service also started, which was destined to outlast all the others. This was Service 72, from Haverhill and Cambridge to Southampton and Bournemouth, and it soon became very popular. Service 6 (Great Chishill - Clacton was extended to start from Royston and the development also began of the successful group of services operated jointly with Yelloway of Rochdale, a respected company with a well-established express network. Yelloway's London routes started from Blackpool and Blackburn, joining at Manchester before they continued southwards, and at Leicester they met Premier Travel coaches on Service 5. Yelloway used Midland Red's Southgate Street coach station, not far from Premier's Red Cross Street stop. A connecting service was advertised for the first time in June 1957, and an important link was thus established. Service 5 now ran daily at Easter and on Fridays to Mondays during the summer, with an overnight journey for those wishing to start their holiday in Clacton with an early breakfast on Saturday. Additional picking-up points were introduced in Birmingham, and over the next few years many more new coach stops were authorised. An application was also made for a service from Oxford to Clacton, but this was contested by Associated Motorways, who were planning a Cheltenham - Felixstowe service. After all the evidence was presented, only the Western Traffic Area was prepared to grant a licence, and it was not taken up at this stage.

A splendid new logo made its appearance in the autumn of 1957. It featured King's College Chapel, probably the most famous building in the city, flanked by a pair of wings and with CAMBRIDGE below. The new device appeared on publicity material and on crews' uniforms, although so far as is known it was never carried on vehicles, and the underlined gold PREMIER TRAVEL fleetname remained unchanged.

Meanwhile the next batch of double-deckers had started to arrive. These were Guy Arabs, the first and only Guys ever owned. Like the Daimlers acquired two years earlier they were wartime vehicles, and by mid-1958 there were ten of these 'no-nonsense' buses in the fleet. One of them (GUF173) began its Premier career in spectacular style when a puncture caused it to overturn

One of the former Southdown Guy Arabs shows the austere lines of its Northern Counties body. Despite their rather basic specification these vehicles served Premier Travel well, returning far better fuel consumption figures than the STLs. All received clear, comprehensive blind displays at the front with the destination and two intermediate points; service numbers were in red on a white background. The rear boxes were mostly left empty. The bus was photographed at Drummer Street on Service 9 from Chrishall. The building on the centre island contained Premier's booking office.

near Thrapston, while on delivery. It was being driven by Chief Engineer Mr Gifford (who was unhurt), and no serious damage was done. There were seven highbridge Guys from Southdown (with GUF registrations), with bodies by Northern Counties and Weymann. Three Roe-bodied lowbridge specimens (CDR748/750/756) came from Plymouth Corporation, and these operated from Haverhill. The Guys had Gardner engines, with a characteristic 'bark', while the basic utility bodies advertised their presence by a metallic rattling sound, which became louder when the buses were ticking over. Despite their lack of sophistication the Guys were reliable machines, and they were in very good condition. Their fuel consumption was far better than that of the STLs, and they served Premier well, although the ex-Plymouth buses were governed down to a degree which made them less lively than the others. All received clear and comprehensive blinds, with the service number (in red on a white background) together with the destination and two intermediate points. The Guys appeared throughout the operating area, replacing most of the STLs and utility Daimlers, although one STL (CXX380) lasted into 1959, while lowbridge Daimler CCX662 soldiered on until the end of 1960. CXX380 was the last wholly pre-war vehicle in the fleet, although another STL (DLU225) survived for several years as a tree cutting vehicle.

The ex-Plymouth Guys were governed down to a degree which made them less lively performers, although they encountered few steep hills on their travels. With its distinctly-lowbridge Roe body, this one is seen departing on its lengthy journey from Cambridge to Kedington. The integration of Services 44/45 had already started but both service numbers continued to appear on blinds until the early 1970s.
Surfleet

A notable withdrawal after the 1957 season was that of Service 65 (Ramsey - Southend), which last ran on 1st September and was the first summer express to disappear. There were no new express services during 1958, although extra stops were introduced on Services 3 and 40. A modest expansion was made on the bus side with the introduction of a local service in Royston. This ran from the Green Man to Icknield Walk/Garden Walk during the afternoons on Wednesdays, Fridays, Saturdays and Sundays(!). With a journey time of just four minutes it was the company's shortest route. It ran as part of Service 16, which also provided a Wednesday link into Royston from Sawston. A surprising development in September saw several increases in the Huntingdon area. Service 17 to Bedford was extended to start from Hemingford Abbotts on Wednesdays and Saturdays, and Service 19 (Huntingdon - St Ives) now terminated at the railway station in St Ives; the rail link between the two towns closed a year later. Service 18 (Godmanchester - RAF Upwood) was revised to provide better connections with Eastern Counties 341 to Peterborough, following the closure of Abbots Ripton station.

An interesting possible purchase which never came about involved a pair of Weymann-bodied AEC Regent IIIs (HER28/29) then being offered for sale by Fison's Pest Control Ltd. Surprisingly, the well-known manufacturer of farm chemicals had bought three such machines new in 1950, for staff transport. These low-mileage buses were in very good condition, but would have added a non-standard type to a double-deck fleet which had just been standardised on Gardner-engined Guy vehicles, and Premier's tender was not accepted. HER28 was acquired by Viceroy Coaches (F C Moore) of Saffron Walden and was later joined by HER27 from the same batch. Both served Viceroy until the mid-1970s, by which time the Premier Travel fleet was entirely AEC.

Delivered in 1959, this was the first new vehicle for nine years and it set new standards for the coach fleet. It also introduced the distinctive 3-panel blind display which was characteristic of Premier's coaches for many years. AEC coaches with Burlingham 'Seagull' bodywork became the standard choice for coaches in the early 1960s and they had replaced all the half-cab coaches by 1964, although this was the only one purchased new. It is seen here at Harston depot ready to perform on the meandering Service 7 to King's Cross. *M J Gifford*

The Regents were not purchased, and fleet additions came in the shape of two Duple-bodied Dennis Lancets (KGY940 and HOM677), continuing a long tradition which started with CCE568. This faithful old vehicle had finally been withdrawn in the previous spring, after twenty years service, and the latest arrivals replaced the other pre-war Lancets, CVE12 and 'The Ant'. Half-cab coaches were now felt to be old-fashioned, and these were the last such additions. Operators now favoured more modern styling, and Premier opted for underfloor-engined vehicles. As an indication of its continuing success, the Company purchased a new coach in July 1959, its first for nine years. UVE333 was an AEC Reliance with Burlingham 'Seagull' bodywork, and by the time it arrived, the express services were all being operated by post-war vehicles. The Midlands - Clacton services continued to expand, with Service 5 running daily except on Wednesdays during the summer. Service 67 now served Parkeston Quay, with an additional Birmingham - Bishop's Stortford journey on Fridays. Two new services also started in 1959. Express Service 73 ran on summer Saturdays from Bedford and Huntingdon to Sheringham, The Runtons and Cromer, the territory of the dying Midland & Great Northern Joint Railway (unkindly known to some as the "Muddle and Go Nowhere"). Very different was a new Service 14, which gave Saffron Walden its own local service for the first time. It was a circular route operating on weekdays, and from this small beginning a network of local routes would develop as the town expanded.

Further secondhand double-deckers arrived. More Daimlers came in June, this time from Maidstone & District. They too had wartime CWA6 chassis, but their original bodies had been replaced in 1948 by much better and very handsome ones by Weymann, with the outswept lower panels which were characteristic of that bodybuilder's products. Premier acquired three

The three Daimler CWA6s acquired from Maidstone & District in 1959 had wartime chassis and 1951 Weymann bodies, with characteristic outswept lower panels. Working on the four-days-a-year May Races service, the bus is seen in the now-pedestrianised Sidney Street in Cambridge. This was the main picking-up point for Eastern Counties local services, including Service 101 with which Premier competed, although there were officially no intermediate stops on the Premier service.

(GKP262/266/656), while several more went to Progressive Coaches of Cambridge, who sometimes hired them to Premier Travel, still in their original dark green and cream livery. Three Bristol K5Gs (BWY979/986/993) arrived at the end of the year, another new make and again with Gardner engines, which had clearly created a good impression. They came from West Yorkshire, and carried post-war ECW bodywork on refurbished pre-war chassis.

And so the 1950s came to a close. They had been eventful years and progress was often far from easy. The size of the fleet had remained at around 40 vehicles, but there had been a steady build-up of routes. The express services now reached an impressive list of destinations stretching from the Midlands to Essex and from Lincolnshire to Hampshire, although the leave services went even further afield. The company did not have things all its own way on the express services, however, and several were subject to restrictions. No local passengers were allowed on Service 5 between Bedford and Northampton, or on the Cambridge - Hitchin section of Service 39.

The brave 1950 bus network was still largely intact, and plans were being made for a town service in Haverhill, although local operations were still restricted in Cambridge, where the licences for the city services were all held by Eastern Counties. Premier Travel buses could carry local passengers on

The first Bristol K5Gs arrived in 1959 from West Yorkshire. Their pre-war chassis had been extensively rebuilt after the war, when they received the lower style of radiator and new ECW bodywork. They resembled the early postwar vehicles still operating for the Tilling fleets in the area, and for a while they gave Premier's routes a 'big bus company' look. This bus was the only one with a three-panel destination layout, although all three number blinds had come adrift when it was seen on Service 9 crossing the main Cambridge-Liverpool Street line near Ickleton in 1964. *G R Mills*

Services 44/45 however, and these did increasingly well as more houses were built along Cherry Hinton Road and in Fulbourn. The Premier services offered a faster ride into the city centre than the competing Eastern Counties 131; this followed a different route to the city centre via Mill Road, which already suffered from traffic congestion. Premier Travel did have one purely local service in Cambridge, but only for a few days each year and officially on a non-stop basis. Recalling Premier's origins within the University, and Mr Lainson's earlier achievements as a rowing man, the former Royal Blue service continued to operate to the college boat races, known as 'The May Bumps' and held annually in June. Buses ran from Sidney Street to the 'Pike and Eel' in Chesterton Fen Road. This was literally on the riverbank, and the service took spectators much nearer to the races than the rival Eastern Counties 101. Operations were during the afternoon on the Wednesday, Thursday, Friday and Saturday of the races, and the service continued until the early 1970s.

One other event at the very end of 1959 must be recorded, for on 27th December Mr W F Matthews died. His faith and optimism had played a great part in the company's growth, and had helped it through the difficult years. Mr Matthews had lived to see Premier Travel become a successful business, and a great sense of loss was felt by everybody in the company.

CHAPTER SIX

CELEBRATION, NEW COACHES, ONE-MAN BUSES

1960-1964

In January 1960 the fleet contained seven different makes of chassis (AEC, Bedford, Bristol, Daimler, Dennis, Guy and Leyland), and numerous styles of bodywork. By the end of the decade it would be far more standardised, although much of interest was still to come. The sixties had yet to start swinging, and most British families still took their annual break at the Great British seaside, although habits were already changing. Britain's first trunk motorway opened in November 1959, and East Anglia had already lost some of its railway lines. It was clear that others were uneconomical, and rail closures soon became regular events. Some of Premier Travel's express services were also becoming less busy, particularly those which started their journeys from small villages in the company's heartlands. Several were extended in an attempt to keep them going, but they all gradually faded away. On the other hand, the long-distance inter-urban services became increasingly important, helped by joint operation with other operators, while the 1960s also saw the start of services to major airports, as air travel was becoming increasingly popular.

Obviously pleased with UVE333, the company acquired three older Burlingham-bodied coaches from Valliant of Ealing. XMT54-56 had the earlier AEC Regal IV chassis with centre-entrance bodywork. They received cast metal Premier Travel fleetnames on their front panels, together with modified destination displays, and it was decided to adopt the AEC/Burlingham combination as the Company's standard coach. Significantly, Daimler CVD6 GCE654 was withdrawn at the end of the summer season, beginning a process which gathered speed over the next few years as the 'new look' spread through the fleet.

Service 5 was still the most important express service, again operating on six days of the week during August. Saturday remained the busiest day, with three journeys from Birmingham in the peak season, together with extra coaches from Leicester and Northampton. More new stops were introduced on the other Midlands - Clacton services. On Service 70 (previously Leicester - Felixstowe direct) bookings were now available to and from Market Harborough and Thrapston as well as Clare, Long Melford, Sudbury, Hadleigh and Ipswich. Service 71 (Worcester - Clacton) gained additional stops on the Baldock - Colchester part in common with those on Service 67 (Birmingham - Harwich). To attract more passengers from the villages, Service 37 now started from Langley Upper Green and was also extended during July and August from Great Yarmouth to Hemsby. Service 66 began its journey to Felixstowe from Fowlmere, and on Saturdays both services were co-ordinated with Service 6 (Royston - Clacton) with an interchange at Saffron Walden. These three services also offered midweek excursions during the summer.

This 1962 scene recalls the days when relief buses were a familiar sight on country bus routes. Former West Yorkshire Bristol K5G BWY985 waits to leave the attractive village of Fowlmere on Service 1, along with an ex-Maidstone & District Daimler CWA6. *G R Mills*

On the bus side, five more Bristol double-deckers arrived, four of them from West Yorkshire (BWY985/988, CWX667, FWX821), with a single example from Hants & Dorset (BTR312). Only one double-decker was withdrawn, this being the surviving utility Daimler (CCX662), which went in November. Its withdrawal followed that of EER99, the last of the Bedford OWBs. There was a small but important addition to the bus network in 1960, for Haverhill had now become large enough to have its own local service. New Service 54 served the growing industrial area on the southern outskirts of the town. There were many route variations, and it sometimes appeared that no two journeys went exactly the same way, but it became increasingly busy as more new housing estates and factories were built, and other town services followed.

The year 1961 was also Premier Travel's Silver Jubilee, an anniversary duly noted in company publicity material, which now carried a photograph of UVE333 in a leafy setting ready for action on Service 5. At the start of the year, services in Royston began using the town's new bus station at The Warren, which replaced the various roadside terminal points previously in use. It was very convenient for the town's market but was built on quite a steep slope, with buses at the exit apparently about to nose-dive onto the A10, and care had to be taken when parking.

Three fleet additions arrived in the spring, and rather surprisingly they were secondhand Bedford OBs with Duple coach bodies (TMM829, GFU700 and MKL51). They were mainly intended for use as one-man buses although they retained their coach seating, and they did not last long. Older Bedford OB bus FER241 was withdrawn, along with former Burgoin's ACF672 (the solitary Thurgood-bodied example), leaving Mulliner-bodied GCE422 as the only Bedford bus in the fleet. Updating of the coach fleet continued, and two more AEC Reliances (138EMF and XHA731) replaced the remaining Daimler (GCE655), and allowed two Leyland PS1 coaches to go (GER140/141). Additional modern coaches were needed for the major express development of the year, when through working was introduced between Clacton and Lancashire. New Services 74 and 75 were operated jointly with Yelloway, following the Service 5 road from Clacton to Cambridge before running direct to Market Harborough and Leicester. The established Yelloway route was then followed to Manchester, after which Service 74 called at Yelloway's coach station in Weir Street, Rochdale before proceeding to Blackburn. Service 75 continued from Manchester to Blackpool, where Yelloway also had their own premises, in Bloomfield Road. The services ran on Friday nights and Saturdays from May to September. A complete journey was something of a marathon in the pre-motorway age, taking nearly 14 hours from Clacton to Blackburn, but valuable new links were provided. There was now no need to change coaches at Leicester, although a change was often necessary at Manchester, Premier's coaches sometimes showing '74/75' as the service number. The timetable also gave details of connecting flights from Blackpool to the Isle of Man. The new services called at Lensfield Road in Cambridge, continuing the tradition of Service 5. This ran daily during the summer, and Premier's position between the Midlands and East Anglia was further strengthened by the provision of still more stops, at Elmdon (Birmingham) Airport and Eaton Socon. Service 70 additionally called at Huntingdon.

Further interest was provided by six more Bristol vehicles, this time from Maidstone & District. Two were Weymann-bodied K6A double-deckers (KKK859/863) for use mainly on contracts, the others being L6A saloons with rear-entrance ECW bodies, the first single-deckers to carry the blue and cream livery. The Bristols all had AEC engines, as did the rebodied Daimlers obtained two years earlier from the same source. One of these (GKP266) came to an untimely end as the Bristols were arriving, when it slid off an icy Fenland road into a drainage channel. It was beyond economic repair and went for scrap, although the other two gave good service for another four years.

The former Colne Valley Railway between Haverhill and Halstead closed on 1st January 1962. For much of its length it ran alongside the main A604 road, used by some of the Clacton services, and by Service 53. The latter previously ran through to Halstead only on Sundays, although the Haverhill - Ridgewell section had been covered on Mondays to Fridays since 1960. It now provided replacement facilities for the railway in conjunction with Eastern National Services 89/89A, with ticket interavailability. Buses terminated at the railway station in Haverhill, which was still served by Cambridge - Sudbury - Colchester trains. There were also bus connections to Cambridge by Eastern Counties 113, while Halstead offered Eastern National and Blackwell's buses to Colchester. This was the first of several rail closures where Premier provided replacement buses, and it came in the year before the publication of Dr Beeching's report, which listed several other local lines for closure.

This rare view shows a Burlingham-bodied AEC Reliance at the Lensfield Road, Cambridge stop used by Services 74/75 when they were introduced in 1961. The new services were something of a marathon, the full journey taking around fourteen hours from Lancashire to Clacton, but they introduced many new direct links. Service 5 and the joint Yelloway services continued to use this stop until the spring of 1963, after which they added to the congestion in Drummer Street. *A J Weir*

This former Maidstone & District Bristol K6A had a Weymann body (with characteristic outswept skirt panels) and was one of a pair purchased in 1961 mainly for contract work, although they occasionally appeared on normal bus services. It was photographed in deceptively rural surroundings at the Pye factory in Chesterton, Cambridge. The Pye contracts began in the early post-war years and were a valuable part of operations, bringing in staff from as far away as Wisbech and Downham Market. Double-deckers were used on a number of contracts until the early 1970s, although this particular bus was withdrawn in 1965. *R A Jenkinson*

The other ex-Maidstone & District buses purchased in 1961 were four L6A saloons. They had Eastern Coachworks bodies and were the only post-war saloons with sliding doors at the rear. They were also the first single-deckers in the blue and cream bus livery, this particular bus having a unique variation with a blue roof. The bus shows its attractive lines at Haverhill depot. *G R Mills*

Leyland PS1 GER834 was withdrawn at the turn of the year, leaving only one Leyland coach in stock. The next batch of double-deckers therefore came as something of a surprise. They appeared early in 1962 in the shape of ten extremely attractive Leyland PD2/3s. New to Ribble in 1950 for limited-stop services, their cream and red livery gave them the name 'White Ladies' (Ribble's ordinary buses wore a mainly red livery). The fully-fronted lowbridge bodywork was by East Lancs, with styling similar to that of the 'County' Daimlers, although the seating was less luxurious. The Leylands had been built with only 49 seats and extra luggage space, but the two single forward-facing seats at the rear of the lower saloon were later replaced by standard bench seats, increasing the capacity to 53. The overhead luggage racks on the nearside downstairs were retained, giving all passengers the chance to bang their heads when leaving their seats. Two sliding windows in the roof made the new arrivals very light and airy upstairs, and folding platform doors were also fitted. Compared to the rattling Guys, the Leylands were a vast improvement, and they soon became a familiar sight. They received neat blinds at the front and rear which managed to squeeze a service number and three lines of route information into the characteristic hexagonal destination boxes. This was very much the age of the double-decker, and for a while there were 25 such vehicles in the fleet, working from all the company's depots.

Further unprofitable journeys were withdrawn from the declining Huntingdon area bus services. Service 17 now ran from The Hemingfords on Saturdays only, and the Tuesday journey on Service 18 now ran only on the third Tuesday of the month between January and March (!) but there was still a late-night journey on Saturdays from Huntingdon to Abbots Ripton. In

Built to a semi-luxury specification for express and limited-stop services, the former Ribble 'White Ladies' were the longest-lived of the secondhand double-deckers. They lasted for over ten years, and were a great improvement on the utility Guys. When delivered they had 'streamlined' embellishments between decks as shown here, but these were soon replaced by advertisements. The bus is in Drummer Street on Service 1. *M Seabrook collection*

contrast, there was now a Monday-Friday journey on Service 20 from St Neots to Huntingdon (returning in the evening as far as Great Paxton), while similar facilities were operated on Service 25 into Huntingdon from the Married Quarters at Gaynes Hall Prison, East Perry. Service 25 continued to serve Great Staughton on Saturdays and was extended during August to Pertenhall. This irregular pattern of operation gives an idea of the low population density in the area, but the services were appreciated by the few passengers who still used them.

The last Leyland coach was withdrawn in April (GER835), but five Dennis Lancets and several Bedford OBs remained in service, along with the ex-Burgoin AEC Regal. Another pair of Burlingham-bodied AEC Reliances arrived in June (XHN573 and 201EMP), and yet another new service between the Midlands and Clacton started in July. This was Service 76 which ran from Kidderminster, Bromsgrove, Redditch, Warwick and Leamington, following the Service 5 route after leaving Northampton. Additional stops were also introduced on Service 5 in villages to the south of Haverhill. The growing Suffolk town now had regular express services to the Midlands and the north-west, as well as to the Essex coast, while the extension of Service 3 provided a direct link with Skegness in summer. Haverhill was also served by London Services 29 and 38, which saw very few changes over the years, although additional stops were introduced in 1962 at Old Harlow and Epping. The express network became increasingly profitable, although the rural bus operations continued to decline. Market-day Service 48 (Brinkley - Haverhill) disappeared early in the following year, at a time when all services experienced a sudden sharp fall in revenue.

Spot the Daimler! The former Ribble Leylands ran for a few years alongside the 'County' Daimlers, giving Premier Travel's bus services a very individual character. The East Lancs bodies on the Leylands were similar in a number of ways to the Wilks & Meade products, although thankfully there were no structural problems with the new arrivals. In this Drummer Street view HVE402 prepares to overake two of the Leylands at the rear of the centre island: this was a regular parking place for Premier vehicles during off-peak periods and between journeys. *M A Sutcliffe*

The winter of 1962-63 was one of Britain's worst, and operations were severely disrupted. On one particularly bad day sixteen buses were abandoned in snowdrifts as crews led stranded groups of passengers home. It was several weeks before things began to return to normal, and this ex-Burgoin Bedford OB was photographed near Helions Bumpstead after the great thaw had started. *A Weir*

The early part of 1963 saw the worst weather for many years, and operations were severely disrupted for several weeks. Roads became impassable, and vehicles frequently failed to start as the fuel froze. It was then necessary to crawl under the vehicles and thaw out the fuel pipes with flares. For six long, cold weeks the staff battled to keep services running. Heaters were not standard features on buses in those days, and the large number of outstationed vehicles had fitters travelling many miles across the desolate, snow-covered Fens at all hours. Not for the first or last time, Premier's loyal staff showed their dedication to the company.

By the end of March things were returning to normal. A notable development was the diversion (at last) of Services 5 and 74/75 to Drummer Street in Cambridge, where they added to the congestion, but provided more convenient facilities for passengers. Service 5 again ran daily from Easter to October, with Saturday still the busiest day. Services 67, 71 and 76 also ran to Clacton during the main holiday season, with the 67 continuing to Harwich as usual and now calling additionally at Bedford and Shefford. Service 71 served Evesham instead of Alcester, and extra stops were introduced south of Haverhill on the 76 in common with Service 5.

The updating of the coach fleet recommenced in the spring and eight more Burlingham-bodied Reliances arrived, including a pair from Yelloway (UDK313/314) and several more from Valliant, one of which (199EMP) unusually retained Valliant's red and grey livery for a while after entering service. More early post-war vehicles departed, including two Bedford OBs, together with the AEC Regal (BGV401), which was written off after an accident at Stretham in which it left the road and severely damaged a house. Other withdrawals saw off Dennis Lancets GER217 and HVE36, once the pride of the coach fleet, and by the end of the year only two Lancets remained. As traditional coaches disappeared, rural express services declined. Saffron Walden became the starting point for Services 37 (Great Yarmouth) and 66 (Felixstowe), with the sections from Langley and Fowlmere discontinued.

Nine former 'private hire' London RFs were Premier's first larger one-man buses, replacing OBs. They retained their curved glass panels but lost their rear destination boxes, which altered their rear profiles quite a lot. Their new livery included a gold Premier Travel fleetname in the LT bullseye at the front, and they replaced double deckers on several timings. These included regular appearances on the Cambridge services, although former RF7 was photographed in Barkway on Service 43. *C W Routh*

Service 6 to Clacton ran from Royston in August and from Great Chishill at other times, connecting with Service 37. Earlier adjustments to the London services resulted in Service 7 becoming a Chrishall - King's Cross operation, with Service 28 now starting from Fowlmere and following a very roundabout route via Newton and Sawston. The Huntingdon area buses saw further cutbacks in October, and only the 20 now had a Monday-Friday service, apart from odd journeys between Huntingdon and Godmanchester on Service 17, with the section from The Hemingfords reduced to a summer Saturday operation. Godmanchester ceased to be an operational depot, and replaced West Wratting as a storage site for withdrawn vehicles.

The year 1964 was an extremely eventful one. On the vehicle side several types disappeared from the fleet, including the surviving Dennis Lancets and Bedford OBs together with all the Bristol single-deckers. The latter had brief careers with Premier, although one of them (LKT993) survived for a while longer as the waiting room at King's Cross Coach Station, still in Premier livery and hiding behind a row of fire buckets. Five Bristol K5Gs also departed, together with AEC Regal IV XMT54, which was withdrawn following serious fire damage.

The decline in the double-deck fleet reflected the reduction in passenger loadings. Following national trends the company saw a solution in one-man operation, referred to by Premier as 'D/C' operation ('driver/conductor'). Some quieter journeys were already worked in this way, using modified Bedford OBs, but in 1964 the first larger one-man buses arrived. These were former London Transport RF-class vehicles of the short 'private hire' variety, built with curved glass panels above the windows for London sightseeing work. Their LUC registrations gave them the nickname 'Lucys', and nine were eventually owned, together with four standard ex-Green Line specimens. The London Transport principle 'good design is good business' seemed very appropriate for these vehicles, which looked very businesslike and soon became familiar on all the bus routes.

The Alexander-bodied AEC Reliances were ideal for the type of work they did and were an immediate success. They greatly enhanced the image of the express operations, although like all Premier's coaches they sometimes appeared on stage services as well. Most of the 49 seats in AVE444B seem to be filled as the coach passes through Milnrow, near Rochdale on one of the joint services to Clacton. Services 77/78 via Northampton were introduced in 1964, although Services 74/75 continued to operate via the original route through Huntingdon. *C W Routh*

The older coaches were replaced by another pair of ex-Valliant Reliances (83/85UME), and by two very special additions. The Directors had taken advantage of recent changes by ordering two new coaches to the new maximum length of 36 feet. The company naturally wished to carry as many passengers as possible, Mr Lainson being especially concerned about "bottoms on seats", and the new coaches were proudly launched in June 1964. They were impressive and eye-catching, with AEC Reliance chassis and Alexander Y-type 49-seat bodywork, registered AVE444B and AVE555B (following on from UVE333, the last new coach). They lacked the curvaceous styling of the Burlingham-bodied coaches, with straight sides and a rather upright front profile. This was emphasised by the destination equipment above the windscreen, but the appearance was helped by the length and by the panoramic side windows. Illuminated 'Premier Travel' panels were fitted on each side and the new coaches looked extremely smart. They were ideal for the type of work they did, and two more were ordered.

Still more new expresses were introduced. Services 77/78 were additional services operated jointly, throughout the year, with Yelloway. Daily coaches were offered from Blackburn (77) or Blackpool (78) to Cambridge, continuing on Fridays, Saturdays, Sundays and Mondays to Clacton. These ran via Bedford and Northampton, while Services 74/75 continued to operate via the more direct route at weekends, calling additionally at Thrapston and Huntingdon and with additional overnight journeys on Saturdays. The joint Yelloway services absorbed most of the Leicester section of Service 5, which became a daily Birmingham - Coventry - Cambridge - Clacton service during the summer, with some journeys using the M1 motorway. The Leicester - Huntingdon - Clacton journeys on Service 5 continued at weekends, with Service 70 (Leicester - Felixstowe) also now serving Cambridge and Haverhill. Following the success of Service 72 to Bournemouth, the company also introduced Service 81 from Haverhill, Linton and Cambridge to Minehead and

When this lightly loaded former Yelloway Reliance was photographed in Baldock on Service 79, there was no indication that this would one day be one of the company's most important routes. When the service started in 1964 there were numerous restrictions. Only pre-booked air passengers could be carried, so that any farewells had to be made in Cambridge! Everyone had to have a ticket, with special rates for children under the age of two. No single tickets could be issued from London Airport to Cambridge and no intermediate stops were allowed. *C W Routh*

Ilfracombe. This took Premier Travel coaches into Devon on a regular basis for the first time, but it was not particularly successful. Still more extensions to existing services took Service 34 on from Skegness to Mablethorpe, while Service 73 now continued along the coast from Cromer to Mundesley.

The other new express services were rather different. The travel agency side of the business was building up rapidly and in January 1964 Premier Travel Agency Ltd had been incorporated as a separate company. In addition, Premier Airlines Ltd had come into being in 1960 as an aircraft handling agent, initially for Derby (later British Midland) Airways, who operated scheduled services from Cambridge to the Channel Islands. Although Derby Airways later pulled out, the flights continued, and agreement was eventually reached for Premier Airlines to have the franchise for this route, under the licence of Guernsey Airlines. A very successful Channel Islands operation was built up, and for several years Premier Airlines was also responsible for holiday flights from Cambridge Airport, under the Air Plan Holidays name. Having become involved with air travel, Premier introduced Service 79 in 1964 after discussions with British European Airways, now part of British Airways. It started with two return journeys from Cambridge to London Airport, as Heathrow was then known. The licence was granted despite objections from Eastern Counties, London Transport and British Railways, but there were numerous restrictions and no intermediate stops were allowed. Although launched in a blaze of publicity the service was not very successful to begin with, and it was soon reduced to one return journey on Fridays, Saturdays, Sundays and Mondays. Loadings then improved slowly, but there was then little indication of how important this route would eventually become. Air travellers from Cambridge were also catered for by Service 80, running on summer Wednesdays to Luton Airport, for holiday flights to and from the Channel Islands. It was not successful, and Luton Airport was not served again until Service 39 (Cambridge - Oxford) was diverted many years later.

The solitary ex-Hants & Dorset Bristol K5G stands beside a virtually identical Eastern Counties bus in Drummer Street, with both vehicles on services to Royston. Following the 1948 agreement, Service 2 had its timetable co-ordinated with that of Eastern Counties 108 (later 146), with ticket interavailability which also applied to common sections of Services 1 and 27. *M A Sutcliffe*

After all this excitement came another rail closure. This affected the line from Audley End to Saffron Walden, where most trains terminated, although a few continued via Ashdon Halt to Bartlow (for Haverhill). The railway closed on 6th September, buses on new Service 59 taking over the following day. Premier operated the through journeys from Haverhill to Audley End Station via Ashdon and Saffron Walden, additionally serving Castle Camps. It followed fairly closely the route of recently-withdrawn Service 57, which had provided market-day facilities during the summer, although the new route did not serve Helions Bumpstead. It also avoided Bartlow, which continued to be served by occasional buses on Service 13 (Abington - Linton - Saffron Walden). Service 59 offered five journeys to Audley End and four back to Haverhill on Mondays to Saturdays only, all connecting with trains to and from Liverpool Street. Additional buses on the Saffron Walden - Audley End section were provided by Viceroy Coaches, with limited participation by Eastern National 301 from Bishop's Stortford. Return and season tickets were interavailable, but less usual was that train tickets could be purchased at normal station prices at the Premier Travel Agency in Saffron Walden, while the bus connections were also shown in railway timetables. Service 59 has continued to run ever since, unlike many rail replacement services which had very short lives.

One other notable event in November 1964 was the closure of Harston depot, where Premier started operations back in 1936 and where major engineering work was still done. As vehicles had become larger the site had become increasingly inadequate, and coaches often had to reverse out onto the busy A10 road. The engineers now moved to the more remote premises at

The former Harston & District premises had been improved considerably since Premier first took over, but the site became increasingly inadequate. The increased length of coaches caused problems, with vehicles having to reverse out onto the busy A10 road. In this view ex-West Yorkshire Bristol K5G BWY979 receives attention, while visible in the background are ex-Maidstone & District Bristol L6A LKT984 and Burlingham-bodied Reliance UVE333. Far more light mileage was necessary after the move to Chrishall, as vehicles now faced a 30-mile round trip from Cambridge for maintenance.

Chrishall, joining the Traffic Department there and leading to a certain amount of friction between the two. Several attempts were made to find a suitable site for a depot in Cambridge, and for a while the company rented some workshop space in Sleaford Street from the Cambridge Co-op, an arrangement which lasted until 1966. Many years would pass before Premier had its own premises in the city, and parking was sometimes difficult, especially on Saturdays. Contract vehicles often spent much of the day at Pye's premises, and a section of the cattle market in Cherry Hinton Road was also used, while a couple of Premier's buses could usually be found resting behind the centre island in Drummer Street during quiet periods. The company also had several reserved spaces in the nearby car and coach park at New Square, although notice to quit had been given in September, as the PSV spaces were needed for additional car parking. Many people felt that New Square would have made a good site for a new bus station, to replace the overcrowded facilities at Drummer Street, but this was not to be.

An exciting year came to an end, and for Premier Travel the sixties had started to go with a swing. There had been a substantial increase in express operations and profits, while loadings on Service 59 far exceeded expectations, the buses carrying more passengers than the trains had done. The fleet also contained two splended new coaches, with another pair on order. It was a time of change and innovation, although some of the company's traditional operations would not survive for much longer, particularly in the Huntingdon area, where the services were now losing one shilling (5 pence) per mile.

COACH EXPANSION, RURAL DECLINE
1965-1970

The second half of the Swinging Sixties saw even more new express services and further updating of the coach fleet, although many rural communities lost their summer holiday services and the bus network declined dramatically.

Two more ex-Yelloway AEC Reliances appeared in January and were notable in being the first to retain their original destination indicators. The last of the ex-London Transport RFs also arrived, one of them (MLL819) running for a short while for Premier still in Green Line livery. Despite the recent arrival of the one-man buses, serious thought was being given to the sale of all the stage services, although one-man conversions had reduced losses, and loadings on the town services were actually improving. Discussions included plans to discontinue seven stage routes, together with London Services 7 and 28, which were now far from busy. The eventual decision was better than expected, for the time being at least, although the two London services disappeared. The ex-Drayton Service 28 now left Fowlmere in a northerly direction and meandered through Sawston, Chrishall, Barkway and Great Hormead, while the former Weeden's Service 7 started from Chrishall and wandered through Duddenhoe End, Langley and Clavering. The services were co-ordinated and the coaches (by then perhaps half full) met in Puckeridge at the Jubilee Cafe. This was the refreshment halt, and it was often possible for one vehicle to take the load on to London. The Service 7 passengers usually transferred onto the Service 28 coach, sometimes accompanied by the conductor, who was shared between the two vehicles. It took ninety minutes to get this far from Fowlmere and a further hour to reach Kings Cross, where facilities were far from palatial. For many years the coaches were small Bedfords; sometimes even a utility would appear, although passengers on Service 28 might be treated to a 'County' Daimler at Christmas and other busy times. The operation was not efficient, using a vehicle and a crew for a whole day with little reward, and the services became increasingly unprofitable. The introduction of modern coaches could not save them, and their withdrawal illustrated the changing character of express operations.

More serious decline was about to set in on the bus side. Although the company retained most of the routes from the great expansion of 1950, several services had disappeared over the years. The Directors now decided to withdraw Services 21 and 22, which had become very infrequent to say the least. Service 21 included the former Service 24 and ran on Thursdays during August from Godmanchester via two different routes to Oundle, the most northerly point reached by Premier's buses. Service 22 linked RAF Upwood with St Ives on Mondays during August, but not on Bank Holiday Monday, and with no local passengers between Kings Ripton and St Ives! Rapidly increasing

The withdrawal of the ex-Weeden and ex-Drayton services to London illustrated the changing character of the express operations. Services 7 and 28 together performed a useful function for many years, offering links from the wide-open spaces between the two main Cambridge-London railway lines. Modern coaches eventually replaced the familiar Bedford OBs, but the services became increasingly uneconomic. Photographed at King's Cross, this coach was one of the three centre-entrance AEC Regal IVs purchased from Valliant of Ealing. *D W Parsons*

car ownership made services like these particularly vulnerable, and it seems surprising that they lasted as long as they did. Other withdrawals (in June 1965) were Services 13 (Abington - Linton - Saffron Walden) and 50 (Haverhill - Withersfield - The Thurlows). These were largely covered by Services 29 and 56, although the Camps End journeys on Service 29 ceased. Amalgamations of surviving services continued, with trunk Services 44/45 combined as Service 44, although there were still several route variations and buses still displayed '44/45'. In an attempt to encourage travel, the company introduced 'Anywhere' tickets. Priced at ten shillings (50 pence) for adults and five shillings (25 pence) for children, they allowed a day's unlimited travel on all the bus routes except the London section of Services 29 and 38. They offered good value provided the traveller did some careful planning beforehand, although they became less useful as further sections of route disappeared.

As country bus routes withered, long-distance express services thrived. Service 5 now operated throughout the year, with a daily Birmingham - Clacton summer service and Leicester - Clacton journeys at weekends. (The winter service ran from Fridays to Mondays via Leicester). On Services 77/78 a daily Lancashire - Cambridge summer service was again provided, continuing to Clacton at weekends. The original routes via Huntingdon (Services 74/75) now operated only on Saturdays, from June to September. Additional Friday journeys were introduced on Service 67, together with an extra stop at Rugby. The summer services to Skegness, Great Yarmouth and Bournemouth still carried heavy loadings, and in Bedford all services now called at the bus station instead of the old stands at St Peter's.

Larger coaches were needed, and two more Alexander-bodied Reliances arrived in the summer. DCE800/801C joined the original pair and gave the company a very impressive 'front line'. The double-deck fleet saw further reductions, and June saw the withdrawal of the ex-Maidstone & District Daimlers, the last vehicles with wartime chassis. The Bristol K6As (KKK859/863) followed in October.

In December the last Burlingham-bodied AEC Reliances arrived: MDK916-918 were older than the other ex-Yelloway vehicles, and they too retained their original indicators. A bigger surprise was the appearance of another double-decker, but only on loan. This was 565CRW, the Alexander-bodied Daimler Fleetline demonstrator, which ran from Chrishall depot for a short while on the Cambridge services, where its red and cream livery caused some confusion. No orders were placed, and the double-deck fleet decreased further as bus loadings continued to decline.

Coaching developments in 1966 revived plans first made nine years earlier for services from Cheltenham and Oxford to Felixstowe and Clacton. The Premier Travel proposal for an Oxford - Clacton service became a reality in May, running from Fridays to Mondays in summer, from Harwich via Clacton, Braintree, Bishop's Stortford, Hitchin and Luton to Oxford. The Associated Motorways plan started as a service from Felixstowe via Ipswich, Colchester, Chelmsford, Harlow, St Albans, Luton and Oxford. Both services continued to Cheltenham, with the Felixstowe variation operating daily throughout the

Various demonstrators were tried, but the only double-decker was this red and cream Daimler Fleetline which ran from Chrishall for a few days in December 1965. Its Alexander body had obvious styling similarities with the new coaches, and it caused quite a stir, although Burwell & District already had two Willowbrook-bodied Fleetlines in service. New double-deckers were not part of the company's plans at the time, however, and no orders were placed. *J R Neale*

year. There were numerous connections and short-workings, and the services were jointly operated. After additional applications by George Ewer (Grey-Green) and Travel House (Luton) Ltd, the four operators agreed that it was better to work together, marketing the new services as 'The Eastlander'. Premier Travel had a 30 per cent share, numbering the Harwich variation as Service 82 and the Felixstowe version 83, although different numbers were shown on the other operators' coaches and in timetables. Cheltenham was then the centre of the Associated Motorways network, where numerous long-distance coaches connected, and the new services provided valuable additional traffic. Applications were also made for services from Bedford to Morecambe and Southport, to be jointly operated with Yelloway, Midland Red and Ribble.

Premier Travel continued to develop its established services. In July, Service 38 was extended further into Suffolk to give Wickhambrook a direct weekend link with London. As the independent enterprise continued, Mr Lainson was elected Chairman of the Passenger Vehicle Operators Association. Maintaining what was now an annual tradition, two more new Alexander-bodied Reliances arrived, registered FCE132/133D. The Lancashire services were increased by the addition of a faster Saturday journey between Bedford and Blackpool, which used motorways between Leicester and Preston and cut journey times by an hour. On Service 72 extra stops were introduced, offering the citizens of Trumpington, Harston, Melbourn and Royston a direct journey to Bournemouth.

Most of the express services started from 1966 onwards were operated in pools with other operators. The famous Eastlander services revived earlier plans for services to Felixstowe and Clacton from Oxford. The services continued to Cheltenham, the hub of the Associated Motorways network with nationwide conections. The service numbers 82 and 83 appeared only on Premier Travel coaches. Service 83 was the more frequent variation, and the coach is shown in Colchester. *W T Canswick*

A remarkable vehicle for a market-day bus service, 'County of Essex' stands at Newmarket on a Tuesday-only Service 56 journey. Towards the end of their lives these vehicles were repainted in the blue and cream livery and confined to local services, normally from Haverhill where their lowbridge layout was useful. All three were withdrawn in 1966 and later scrapped.

Significant withdrawals during 1966 were the 'County' Daimlers (HVE401-403). These notable vehicles were now confined to local stage services, but they continued to attract attention and retained their coach seating, despite being painted in bus livery and adorned with advertisements. One of them (HVE401) stood disused at Godmanchester for a while, but all three were eventually scrapped; it is a great pity that none were saved for preservation. Their withdrawal eliminated Daimlers from the fleet.

A further cut from the bus network came at the end of September when the Hitchin section of Service 12 was finally withdrawn. In its final form it consisted of one return journey, in summer, from Saffron Walden. Service 12 continued to operate between Saffron Walden and Chrishall on weekdays, with market-day extensions to Royston.

Rather surprisingly an additional double-decker joined the fleet early in 1967, in the shape of DCK219, another ex-Ribble Leyland. Since leaving the Ribble fleet it had been with Reliance of Newbury, and it now began a further six years work for Premier. The ex-Ribble vehicles continued to appear on the busiest bus routes, comparing very favourably with newer vehicles in neighbouring fleets. By the end of 1967 the Leylands were Premier's only

The Hitchin section of the marathon Service 12 was withdrawn in September 1966. In its final form this consisted of a Tuesday return journey from May to September. Service 12 continued to serve Chrishall on weekdays, with market day extensions to Royston. The journeys from Kelshall and Therfield into Royston were now provided by the coaches of H V Richmond of Barley, who also ran part of the Royston town service. FWX821 was the only postwar Bristol K5G and it is seen here with other Premier vehicles at Saffron Walden before new blinds were fitted. *M Seabrook collection*

This 'White Lady' joined the Premier fleet after service with Reliance of Newbury, who had no further use for it following the sale of their stage services to Thames Valley. It differed from the others in several ways: it was still only a 49-seater (the same capacity as the new single deck coaches!), its rear indicator had been panelled over and was not restored and at some stage in its wanderings it had lost its front bumper, making it instantly recognisable from a distance.

double-deckers, following the withdrawal of the surviving Bristol K5Gs. These had the last pre-war chassis in the fleet, and the final one (CWX667) was a regular performer on the busy Haverhill town services. Premier was fortunate in being the sole operator of local services in a town which was still expanding, and as well as the original Service 54 (Western Avenue - Hollands Road Industrial Area) there was now a circular Service 57, serving the large new Clements Estate. The influx of Londoners also assured the future of Service 38, but despite its growth Haverhill lost its railway service in March 1967, with the closure of the Shelford - Sudbury section of the Cambridge - Colchester line. Replacement buses were provided between Haverhill and Sudbury by Theobald's of Long Melford, and between Cambridge and Haverhill by Eastern Counties, who provided extra journeys (numbered 413) on their existing 113 route. The closure of the railway left Premier Travel as the only provider of through Cambridge - Colchester trips, with several express services over this section. Bus connections continued to be available at Halstead.

The National Coach Rally at Blackpool took place in April, and Premier Travel entered one of the previous year's AEC Reliances, FCE132D. It was the first time an Alexander-bodied vehicle had appeared at the Blackpool event, and the coach (with Driver H. Law) was the subject of much favourable comment, although no awards were forthcoming. Another two Alexanders joined the fleet during the summer, registered GER501/502E. One of these (GER501E with Driver H. Lee) became a regular performer on Service 5, which became a daily Birmingham - Clacton operation, continuing to Parkeston Quay, Dovercourt and Harwich on Fridays and returning on Mondays. Harwich was still reached by Service 67 on summer Saturdays, and Premier Travel coaches could also be seen in the Essex port on Eastlander Service 82 (to Cheltenham) and also on Service 87. This was a new route, operated jointly with Midland Red on summer Saturdays and Sundays, which provided still more journeys from and to the Midlands. It followed the Service 67 roads to Northampton before continuing along the Service 76 route to Warwick. In Birmingham it avoided Digbeth, calling instead at stops to the south of the central area, and after passing through Shrewsbury and Wrexham, the final section took the coach through a string of north Wales resorts between Rhyl and Llanfairfechan before it finally arrived in Bangor. It was another marathon route, with a scheduled journey time of over 13 hours, and it brought Premier Travel coaches regularly into Wales for the first time.

Also new was Service 84, from Birmingham via Cambridge to Southend-on-Sea, not served by the company's express coaches since the withdrawal of Service 65 from Ramsey in 1956. The new service ran on five days of the week and was operated jointly with Midland Red (further strengthening the good working relationship which the two operators enjoyed) and also initially with Eastern Counties (Service Y) and Eastern National.

Premier Travel and Midland Red also became joint operators (along with Yelloway and Ribble) on the routes from Bedford to Morecambe (Service 85) and Southport (Service 86). Premier and Yelloway had a joint 75 per cent share on these services, although the Southport variation was very short-lived. The network was becoming ever larger, with thirty different express services advertised during the summer of 1967, as well as the usual range of excursions. Joint working was a feature of all the new services, as operators increasingly realised that there was little to be gained by automatically opposing each others' applications.

A typical market day scene at Royston bus station in the late 1960s. A group of Premier staff discuss a matter of importance, as former Green Line LYF448 (ex-RF97) departs on a Service 12 journey to Chrishall via Shaftenhoe End with a healthy load, despite its rather uninformative destination! Former Valliant Reliance 86UME waits to depart on Service 16 to Sawston, while in the background a United Counties Bristol LS approaches on the Buntingford-Biggleswade service, part of which later passed to London Country. *C W Routh*

More modest increases to the express operations came with the introduction of new stops on existing services. Service 79 to London (Heathrow) Airport could now pick up pre-booked airline passengers in Royston and Baldock, while London Services 29 and 38 called at Stansted and Bishop's Stortford. Despite the growth, further pruning was necessary. The extension of Service 3 to Haverhill had not been successful, and Service 6 (Royston - Clacton) ran for the last time at the end of the season. The single journey on Service 35 (Clacton - King's Cross) did not reappear, and the leave services were discontinued as the aerodromes closed. Express Service 8 (RAF Duxford - Cambridge) was withdrawn, replaced by Service 1 which by that stage had all but ceased to serve its traditional terminus at Royston. The married quarters at RAF Duxford continued to provide traffic, but passengers now had a much longer journey to and from Cambridge. The closure of RAF Upwood led to further cuts in the Huntingdon area.

The arrival of more new vehicles, and the departure of the Bristol double-deckers, meant that Premier Travel ended 1967 with its most standardised fleet ever, comprising 11 Leyland PD2/3 double-deckers and 44 AEC single-deckers (8 Alexander-bodied Reliance coaches, all bought new, 23 Burlingham-bodied Reliance coaches, from a variety of sources, and 13 Regal IV buses).

From 1st January 1968 there was an important expansion to the express operations. On the previous day passenger traffic had ceased on the Cambridge to Bedford and Bletchley to Oxford sections of the Cambridge to Oxford railway line. Service 5 and the joint Yelloway services passed through Cambridge and Bedford, but local passengers had to use the long United Counties bus route (128) which continued to Northampton. A new limited-stop bus service (428) started, between Cambridge and Bedford, jointly operated by Eastern Counties and United Counties. It passed through the area formerly served by the railway and it had a short life. Premier Travel provided replacement facilities for the trains between Cambridge and Oxford. Operations on Service 39 had increased slowly and now linked the two cities throughout the year on Fridays, Saturdays and Sundays via Luton and Aylesbury. The route was still worked jointly with Percival's Motors (Cambridge) Ltd, whose associate company, Percival's Motors (Oxford) Ltd, also provided a Cambridge - Oxford service via Buckingham and Bicester. All three operators now participated in a joint service on the Luton route, which received a railway subsidy and called additionally at the railway stations in Cambridge and Oxford. Two daily journeys were provided, with an extra coach on Fridays and Saturdays. It was only a rail-replacement service between the terminal points, but it benefited by serving a far more populated area in between than the trains had done. Service 39 became increasingly important, although there were still some restrictions on local journeys to begin with.

In May, changes were made to the Heathrow Airport service (79), following discussions with Eastern Counties, who had been one of the objectors when the service started. It now became a joint operation with the larger operator, with the number of daily journeys increased to two. One of these started at Peterborough and called additionally at Huntingdon on its way south; an additional stop at Alconbury was later added. The only stops after leaving Cambridge were at Royston and Baldock, and coaches served Terminals 1, 2 and 3 at Heathrow Airport. Although the service was still intended for airline passengers, they could now be accompanied by "persons wishing to see their departure or meet their arrival".

Further unprofitable mileage was withdrawn. The section of Service 37 beyond Great Yarmouth to Hemsby did not reappear in the summer of 1968, and Service 73 ran to Mundesley for the last time at the end of the season. Further RAF cutbacks led to the withdrawal of the Stradishall section of Service 44, and for the next fifteen years the two outer terminal points for this service were Kedington and Withersfield. Service 52 (RAF Stradishall - Haverhill) had already disappeared, but this section continued to be served by Services 38 and 55. In Saffron Walden the recently-introduced Service 15 to Whiteshot Way also ceased, later to reappear as part of Service 14.

The coach fleet was increasingly busy, and modernisation continued. Although the Burlinghams were not the oldest vehicles in the fleet, they had nearly all been obtained secondhand, and were now past their prime, with high

The six ex-Northern General Reliances were the first Harrington-bodied vehicles in the fleet, and they unusually ran in their original cream and red livery for a while. These vehicles had fewer seats than the 41-seat Burlinghams they replaced, but their styling was more modern and they were only eight years old when purchased. This January 1969 scene at Chrishall shows the effects of winter weather on the livery. Most were sold for further service after fairly short careers with Premier. *C W Routh*

mileages and rather dated styling. The interiors of some were also becoming shabby, a notable example being 772EMU, which was confined to school contracts unless some dire emergency arose! Replacements came in the shape of more Reliances, whose stylish Harrington 'Cavalier' bodywork introduced a new coachbuilder to the fleet. Six of these vehicles arrived at the end of 1968, from Northern General. Their 37-seat capacity did not quite match that of the Burlinghams they replaced, which was interesting in view of the decision to order the next new coaches to the recently authorised 12-metre length. In November 1967 the local press had reported that "the longest coaches in Britain" would soon join the Premier Travel fleet, removing the need to provide relief coaches for a few extra seats. Despite their relatively low seating capacity, however, the ex-Northern General coaches were a good purchase, providing a more modern image at a time when coaching activities were increasing. A Northern General Albion Aberdonian saloon was also inspected, but the Directors were unimpressed and none were purchased.

While Premier was building up its express services and rationalising its bus network, a Labour government returned to power. Nationalisation again became a topical issue, and the 1968 Transport Act took effect from 1st January 1969. Its provisions included the amalgamation of the Transport Holding Company (which had taken over the nationalised BTC operators) with the British Electric Traction group to form the National Bus Company, the largest bus company in the world. There had been strong opposition to the takeover from several BET companies, including Midland Red. Premier Travel was now surrounded by NBC operators, for Eastern Counties, Eastern National and United Counties were all included and were later joined by London Country Bus Services, which took over the Country Area of London Transport at the start of 1970. However, there was no immediate, visible change and the companies all carried on as before. There was no compulsory nationalisation of existing independents, who continued to work alongside the NBC subsidiaries. However, one very old-established independent did disappear, for in September 1969 the remaining Birch Brothers services in the Bedford area were taken over, mainly by United Counties. The Birch coach operations later passed to Grey-Green.

The 1968 Act also introduced grants towards the purchase of new buses, as well as allowing local authorities to subsidise socially-necessary services which were unprofitable and which would otherwise be withdrawn. The provision of grants for new vehicles would later be very useful to Premier Travel, while council support for marginal bus services meant that some of the loss-making mileage could continue to operate, and discussions began with local authorities. These came too late to save several long-established services, and large-scale cuts were planned, although some sections were later reinstated as County Councils became more involved with supporting local bus services.

The long-awaited new coaches were delivered in May 1969, giving the company further valuable publicity. Outwardly similar to the Alexander-bodied Reliances already in stock, LJE991/992G were actually three feet longer, with seats for 53 passengers instead of 49. Their arrival followed the extended loan of several Ford Thames coaches, which appeared on bus, express and contract work. Four with Plaxton Embassy bodies (EPT940/2/3/4B) were operated in the blue livery of Trimdon Motor Services. Three older specimens followed, from various sources, with Duple and Burlingham bodywork. All compared very unfavourably with Premier's AECs.

An indication of the type of coach operated by many independents in the 1960s, this Duple-bodied Ford Thames was one of several long-term hires early in 1969. These lightweight vehicles had lorry-derived chassis and compared unfavourably with Premier's AEC Reliances, a type more usually associated with larger operators. Seven Fords were hired, and this one was photographed in Braintree. *G R Mills*

Opposite top Three 36-foot Reliances with luxurious Harrington bodies seating only 45 were obtained in 1969 from Whyte's of Ashford, indicating that Harrington bodies were to become a feature of the fleet. Their luxurious seating made them useful private-hire coaches, but this one was photographed on a Service 5 Clacton-Leicester journey. Many more Harrington-bodied Reliances were subsequently purchased. *C W Routh*

Opposite centre This was one of nine former Devon General Reliances, whose Weymann bodies unusually had sliding external cab doors as well as internal ones. The spacious nature of the cabs also allowed one driver to bring his dog to work with him. Devon General's blue interior scheme fitted in very well with Premier's livery, and the solid, well-built bodies stood up well to the rigours of country bus work. The bus is seen leaving Haverhill in November 1969 on Service 58 to Braintree, which was discontinued a year later. *G R Mills*

After giving homeward-bound Pye workers a taste of their riding qualities, the impressive new vehicles settled down on the joint Yelloway services (74/75 and 77/78). Together with other services to Northampton, these now called at Derngate Bus Station, having previously stopped in Campbell Square. Despite the need for larger coaches on these services, withdrawals of other express facilities continued. Service 37 to Great Yarmouth now started from Haverhill, although a connection to and from Saffron Walden was provided on Saturdays by Service 38. Service 66 to Felixstowe started from Saffron Walden on Tuesdays only, the Friday and Saturday journeys commencing at Haverhill. Service 3 ran direct from Cambridge to Fenstanton on its way to Skegness, no longer serving Histon, Cottenham and other villages to the north of the city. The end of the 1969 season also saw the complete withdrawal of Service 36 (Ramsey - Great Yarmouth) and Service 70 (Leicester - Felixstowe). Leicester was now left entirely to Services 77/78 for the winter, with Service 5 running direct from Coventry to Northampton. The winter service also continued to Harwich for the first time, and now ran on three days of the week. Service 5 was continuing to increase slowly but surely.

Three Harrington-bodied Reliances (631-633WKL) arrived at the end of the year, with luxurious 36-foot bodies seating only 45. They came from Whyte's of Ashford, and many more secondhand Harringtons would follow.

Discussions had meanwhile continued over the future of the bus network, and one-man operation was seen as the way forward. Nine Weymann-bodied AEC Reliances (with VDV registrations) from the Devon General fleet started to replace the RFs. Unlike their predecessors the Reliances had manual gearboxes, which Premier continued to specify for many years afterwards. They were also 8 feet wide, as opposed to 7 feet 6 inches, which was not really an advantage on the narrow roads they served. Despite the company's experience with AEC products, the AV470 engines were more troublesome than had been expected, but several lasted until 1976.

Although some local authorities were willing to pay subsidies, large-scale cuts were now essential if services were to continue, and rationalisation took place in stages during 1970. Some services were withdrawn completely, others had uneconomic sections discontinued. Timetable cuts reduced the number of journeys and the days of operation, and more services became seasonal.

The major cuts (which also allowed more efficient use of vehicles) were:

Service
10 Elmdon - Arkesden section withdrawn.
12 Chrishall - Royston section withdrawn, including journeys via
    Shaftenhoe End.
16 Sawston - Royston section to operate May to September only.
17 St Neots - Bedford section withdrawn.
23 Service withdrawn (Sawston - Saffron Walden, Tue).
25 Service withdrawn (Great Staughton - Huntingdon, Sat).
26 Royston - Barley section withdrawn, also journeys via Nuthampstead.
    To operate Thursdays and Saturdays only.
27 Service withdrawn (Barkway - Fowlmere - Cambridge, Fri).
29 Kedington - Linton and Saffron Walden - London sections withdrawn.
    To operate Tuesdays only.
49 Weston Colville - Newmarket section withdrawn. To operate Fridays only.
53 Ridgewell - Halstead section withdrawn. Entire service withdrawn
    Sundays.
58 Service withdrawn (Haverhill - Braintree, Wed).
60 Service withdrawn (Haverhill - Kedington circular, Sat).

Some sections of route were not lost entirely, but were covered by other services. For example, Service 43 (Chrishall - Barley - Barkway - Royston) continued to serve villages no longer reached by Services 12 and 26, while most of Service 27 had been absorbed over the years by Service 1 (Royston - Fowlmere - Cambridge), which followed several different routes between Newton and Cambridge.

Amidst all the cuts, another new town service started in Haverhill, Service 52 providing four buses on Mondays-Fridays to and from the new Chalkstone estate. Plans were also made to extend the local journeys provided in Royston on Service 16. A weekday service was planned, with buses serving the railway station and York Road industrial area, but nothing came of the proposals.

Service 29 ceased to be an express service, Service 38 providing a daily Haverhill - King's Cross service which reached Kedington at weekends. This service also called at Stansted Airport in summer, for pre-booked passengers. Other express changes saw Service 4 extended to start from Huntingdon to cover for withdrawn Service 36. Service 5 ran daily from Birmingham to Harwich, with Saturday journeys from Leicester to Clacton via Kettering and Huntingdon. The original Birmingham - Harwich service (67) had now been reduced to a Rugby - Clacton, while Services 37 and 66 started from Haverhill.

Still more AEC Reliances joined the fleet; OVE232/233J had Alexander 53-seat bodies, while unexpected additions were five Duple-bodied examples from York Brothers of Northampton. One (83BNV) was a front-entrance 43-seater, the others (YBD79-82) having unusual centre-entrance 41-seat bodywork. Painted in all-over Premier blue, they sometimes appeared as crew-operated buses, as well as on coach work. More Burlinghams departed, notably UVE333 after severe accident damage. By December the RFs had also gone, although only one double-decker (DCK218) was withdrawn. Some timings were still felt to be "decker jobs", and conductors continued to be employed, although their future was now uncertain, as indeed was the future of many independent bus and coach operators. The fledgling National Bus Company was about to make its corporate presence felt, and far-reaching changes were imminent.

Above The only one of the Cambridge routes to disappear in 1970 was the former Drayton's Service 27. In its final form this consisted of a Friday-only return trip from Barkway, but it had once stretched as far as Little Hadham, where a vehicle was outstationed for the service. Surrounded by a selection of typical Eastern Counties vehicles of the period, one of the ex-Maidstone & District Daimlers approaches Drummer Street on the service several years earlier. This bus was actually withdrawn in November 1961, after it slid off an icy Fenland road into a drainage channel. *A B Cross*

Centre The five Reliances purchased from York Brothers of Northampton in 1970 had Duple bodywork, a make not favoured for many years, and their rounded styling made them look rather dated alongside the Alexanders and Harringtons. Four of them dated from 1961 and had 'Britannia' bodies with centre entrances, the last such vehicles purchased, and they sometimes appeared with two-person crews on the stage routes. This one is seen at Haverhill on one of the town services in November 1970. The destination blinds on these coaches were very rarely used. *G R Mills*

Left New to York Brothers in 1962, this coach was the only one purchased with the later style of Duple 'Britannia' body with a front entrance. It was photographed in September 1971 at Bedford bus station, the blind offering no clues as to its activities! Most of the former York coaches were sold after just over three years with Premier Travel. *C W Routh*

CHAPTER EIGHT

BUS GRANT, NEW IMAGE
1971-1975

Following the bus cuts, the next few years saw the emphasis move increasingly towards express coach operation. The appearance of the fleet would also change, although there was no indication of this in 1971.

Early in the year came the changeover to decimal currency. Premier's fares went over to the new system on 15th February, with tickets now printed to show '10p' and '1p' instead of 'SHIL'S' and 'PENCE'. Notices appeared in buses stating the company's willingness to accept pre-decimal coins in multiples of six old pence (2.5p). A fares increase in May affected several services in Haverhill, Royston, Saffron Walden and Huntingdon for the first time in five years. Off-peak returns were introduced on the Cambridge services where, as usual, fares were increased in line with those of Eastern Counties. This company was facing difficulties at its Cambridge depot, with traffic congestion and staff shortages beginning to cause serious problems. An eight-week overtime ban in support of a pay claim caused many cancellations in December 1970, and a total strike for three days followed early in 1971. This generated little sympathy for the crews, but provided increased loadings for Premier Travel, whose services into Cambridge all overlapped with those of Eastern Counties. None of the local independents suffered from staff shortages, and traffic delays were less of a problem to their largely rural operations.

The express network became even larger in 1971 with the takeover of the Dunstable - Glasgow licence of Buckmaster of Leighton Buzzard. This became Service 88, operating on Friday nights from Dunstable, Luton and Bedford to Lesmaghow, Hamilton and Glasgow, where the coach spent Saturday before returning south on Sunday morning. On at least one occasion a Premier vehicle performed a local sightseeing tour for Western SMT, later a joint operator on the service. There were initially no single-ticket facilities available from Scotland; a similar restriction applied to Service 72 from Bournemouth.

There were few changes to the other summer services, although Eastern National ceased to participate on Service 84 (Birmingham - Southend). More significant changes were made to Service 79. This continued to be operated jointly with Eastern Counties, but from 1st August the unsuccessful Peterborough extension was withdrawn. Additional stops were introduced at Mill Hill, South Harrow and Hayes, and at Heathrow the coach no longer called at all three terminals, running instead to the Central Bus Station. The service was no longer restricted to airline passengers and their friends, and children under two no longer needed a ticket. This section of the faretable had a slightly bizarre look to it: for example, the price of an adult period return from Royston to Heathrow was £1.90, but an additional outlay of 19p was necessary if a baby was being carried. A real bargain for any youngster able to appreciate such things!

Secondhand AEC Reliances with Harrington bodies were regularly purchased during the early 1970s, and together with the new Alexander-bodied vehicles they saw off all the older coaches. The two Harrington-bodied Reliances purchased from Bowen's in 1971 had the later 'Grenadier' style of bodywork, and this one was photographed in the following year at Colchester. The coach is in the early stages of its marathon journey from Harwich to Bangor on Service 87, which was operated jointly with Midland Red. Several of the Harringtons received blinds from withdrawn Burlingham-bodied coaches, but none ever received modified indicator displays as the Burlinghams had done. *G R Mills*

With still more coaches needed, seven more Harrington-bodied Reliances arrived, including four from Valliant and two from Bowen's of Birmingham (BOF854/855C) with the later 'Grenadier' body style. They saw off the last of the ex-Yelloway Burlinghams (UDK311-314).

Attention turned in the spring of 1972 to the bus fleet, where the Leylands were nearing the end of the road. Not unexpectedly, the replacement vehicles continued the association with AEC products, and eight rather inelegant Park Royal/AEC Bridgemasters (with reversed-NJO registrations) arrived from City of Oxford, who had repainted them in Premier livery. They were the largest double-deckers so far operated, with 65 seats and forward entrances. The heaters and low entrance steps were welcome features, but the AECs lacked the refinement of the Leylands, some of which soon returned to front-line duties following damage to the new-fangled Bridgemasters by overhanging branches. The low-height design allowed centre gangways on both decks, however, and they were the first such vehicles to operate regularly from Haverhill, although the offending bridge had now been removed. The Bridgemasters did not last long, most staying for only two or three years. They usually covered the busier workings on the Cambridge services (1/2/9/44) and the Haverhill town services (52/54/57), with regular interworking at Haverhill onto Services 42, 55 and 56, although they sometimes strayed onto other routes, and initially also appeared on contracts. Only seven entered service, the eighth (328NJO) spending its entire career at Chrishall depot.

Eight of these rather ungainly Park Royal/AEC Bridgemasters were purchased from City of Oxford in 1972. Their internal layout was better than the awkward lowbridge arrangement of the Leylands, but their fibreglass front domes were no match for overhanging trees. The rear air suspension was also of little benefit on country lanes while the shock absorbers often failed, and a ride on one of these buses was a nosiy, bouncy experience. The forward entrance and two-man crew are clearly visible in this view, taken at Haverhill Road Corner in Stapleford on one of the short Service 9 journeys. *G R Mills*

Coaching developments continued, and another fast Blackpool journey was introduced on summer Saturdays, this time from Cambridge. It followed a more direct route between St Neots and Market Harborough, calling at Kimbolton, Rushden, Wellingborough and Kettering. It also used motorways between Leicester and Preston, cutting the journey time from Cambridge by nearly two hours. Other changes left Oxford railway station unserved by Service 39, but the Cambridge station stop remained in use, with train connections shown in the coach timetable. The Mablethorpe extension of Service 34 from Bedford ran for the last time in September, while the few remaining buses on Service 53 (Haverhill - Ridgewell) ceased in the same month. Service 1 had meanwhile ceased to serve Royston, and buses now ran in service between Chrishall and Duxford Aerodrome or Fowlmere.

Premier Travel's regular bus passengers often commented on the age of the vehicles they travelled in, a situation which was now about to improve dramatically. The 1968 Transport Act encouraged operators to modernise their fleets by providing grants towards the cost of new buses. The Bus Grant Scheme was originally intended to last until 1975, but in 1971 the now-Conservative government increased the grant from 25 per cent to 50 per cent, and extended the scheme until 1980. Some of the previous rigid specifications were relaxed, and the 'grant coach' made its appearance. To qualify for the grant, new coaches had to be have design modifications to make them suitable for use as one-man buses. It was quickly realised that Premier, with its express and stage services, could benefit from the scheme, and the next two Reliances were ordered to grant specification.

The beginning of the end for Premier's conductors. One of the first two Alexanders to bus-grant specification is seen here at Chrishall soon after entering service in October 1972. As well as the revised front-end styling the new vehicles featured two-leaf driver-controlled doors instead of the one-piece manual doors fitted to the coaches. There were also cash trays and other fittings for one-man working, while new Setright Speed ticket machines were a feature, although the older Insert machines remained in use on other vehicles for the time being. *G R Mills*

They materialised as VER261/262L, and like the previous two pairs they were 12-metre 53-seaters. The Alexander bodywork featured revised front-end styling together with driver-controlled doors and fittings for one-man working. They entered service in the autumn as one-man buses, on timings previously worked by double-deckers; their seating capacity was felt to be sufficient in view of the declining number of passengers using the bus services. New Speed Setright ticket machines were also introduced, following the use of a secondhand Speed Setright on the Haverhill town services, although the older Insert machines continued in use on other vehicles.

The new vehicles had to operate 50 per cent of their total mileage in their first five years on stage carriage services. (This was later modified to 50 per cent in each calendar year). The 1968 Act redefined these as services with fares below one shilling (5p). These services qualified for fuel tax rebate, and several operators now redefined short sections of express routes as stage carriage operations. Local fares were accordingly introduced on the Haverhill - Halstead section of Services 5 and 77/78, covering the recently-withdrawn Service 53. The well-informed (and brave) traveller could now flag down a Clacton-bound coach at, say, Baythorne End and ask for a ticket to Sible Hedingham or Halstead. How many took advantage of this is not known but the Act certainly helped Premier to recoup some of its operating costs and to obtain modern vehicles, and as 1972 ended there were clear indications of what was to follow. By then only two Leylands remained, most having gone to a scrapyard near Duxford Aerodrome, where they were easily visible to passengers riding past on the replacement Bridgemasters, or the new Alexanders.

On 1st January 1973, Premier Travel Services Ltd was formed as the trading company for the bus and coach part of the Premier Travel Group, leaving Premier Travel Ltd as the parent holding company. There was no visible change to the vehicles at this stage. On the same day Service 52 (Haverhill Market Hill - Chalkstone Way) was extended further into the growing Chalkstone Estate. Less welcome was the withdrawal from 10th February of the remaining section of Service 17 (Godmanchester - Huntingdon - Buckden - St Neots), although partial replacement facilities were provided by Service 20 (Huntingdon - Godmanchester - The Offords - St Neots).

In March the surviving Leylands (DCK208/217) departed, and at long last the fleet contained vehicles of just one make. All vehicles in stock were now AECs, and except for the double-deckers all were Reliances, albeit of several different lengths and with a variety of bodywork, ranging from the 1957 former Devon General buses to the latest grant coaches. It had long been the intention to operate an all-AEC fleet, and providing spare parts was now much simpler than it had been ten years earlier, when six makes of chassis were represented. Further Harringtons arrived, bringing the total to nineteen. They included the last of many coaches from Valliant-Cronshaw (as this operator had now become), registered MMX103-105C. They saw off the surviving Burlinghams, which had come from the same source several years earlier. These handsome coaches had played a valuable part in building up the express network, although in their final years they rarely appeared on long-distance services.

Change seemed to be everywhere in the bus and coach world. At the end of 1972, the National Bus Company unveiled its new standard bus liveries of poppy red or leaf green, both with white relief. Coaches in NBC fleets started to appear in the all-white scheme, which would soon become so widespread. Premier Travel also unveiled a new livery in August 1973, when the long-familiar and unusual Premier blue with dark blue or cream relief was superseded by two brighter shades, known as electric blue and royal blue. A new, circular logo incorporating two arrows replaced the winged motif, (which had been simplified in 1962), and appeared on coaches and publicity material. Two more Alexander-bodied grant coaches were delivered in the new scheme; XVE814/815L reverted to the 36-foot length and were 49-seaters, but were otherwise similar to the previous pair. Secondhand arrivals in the new colours were six Reliances (with BVO-C registrations) from Barton of Nottingham. Their 51-seat Harrington Grenadier bodies were equipped for one-man bus work, and they were useful dual-purpose additions. Early repaints were recently-acquired MMX104C (on which various other colours had been tested) and Alexanders FCE132D and OVE233J; the latter also acquired the new-style front end, but retained its original manual door. Repainting proceeded steadily, although the new livery was not applied to the remaining Burlinghams, or to the ex-Northern General and ex-York Brothers coaches.

The National Bus Company had meanwhile been finalising its plans to change the face of coach travel. In October, National Travel was launched to co-ordinate the express services of the NBC operators. The white National coach was already a familiar sight, and established express services now received three-figure service numbers on an area basis. The new numbers appeared on Premier Travel routes which were jointly-worked with National, so that coaches to Heathrow Airport now showed 079, a notable use of the Premier service number. Eastlander Services 82/83 became 182/183, while other routes renumbered were Services 84 (499), 85 (517) and 87 (087);

The country bus and its competitors at Bishop's Stortford. The second pair of bus-grant Alexanders were the first new vehices to carry the revised livery introduced in 1973. By this stage the Bishop's Stortford services were a self-contained operation worked by just one single decker, which was now sufficient for the loads carried. This was very different from the situation of a few years earlier, when several double-deckers were necessary on market days. The future of Services 10 and 26 was uncertain, and the blinds of the new vehicles did not include displays for these services. *K Lane*

Repainting of older coaches into the new livery proceeded steadily, although many people regretted the passing of the earlier, more distinguished shade of blue. The coach was photographed leaving the Beach Coach Station, Great Yarmouth on the long-familiar Service 4 with Driver Fred Barker, who completed 45 years service with Premier Travel. *C W Routh*

subsequent joint services also received National numbers. Premier's other express services continued to reach the parts the white coaches did not reach, at least not via the same routes, and the distinctive liveries of Premier, Yelloway, Percival's and others provided welcome splashes of colour in a sea of corporate white. The long-standing arrangements with NBC operators also continued, and it was still possible to book on Service 5 in the offices of Midland Red, United Counties and Eastern National, even though these companies were now parts of the new giant.

In December, it was decided to withdraw the remaining Huntingdon area bus services. These were now reduced to Service 18 (Huntingdon - Upwood circular, Saturdays); Service 19 (Huntingdon - Godmanchester - St Ives, Mondays/Saturdays) and Service 20 (Huntingdon - Godmanchester - St Neots, Thursdays/Saturdays), with one or two round trips on each. Loadings had become very poor, and after a long, slow decline the services quietly passed into history. Premier Travel coaches still served Huntingdon, and Whippet Coaches continued the tradition of independent bus operation in the area, although most of the former Premier services were covered by United Counties.

As if to emphasise the new look, the ex-York Bros coaches had all departed by the spring of 1974, and they were followed by the former Northern General vehicles, the first Harringtons to go. Most of these saw further service with other operators, but as far as Premier was concerned they were too small. Further new Alexanders to grant specification arrived in May (OJE550/551M), along with two more Harringtons (HLP10/11C), the last to be purchased. They came from the immaculate Surrey Motors fleet, and were of the standard type with manual doors.

Premier Travel coaches reached Liverpool in the spring, on new Service 90, operated jointly with Yelloway and National Travel. The National contribution was provided by Crosville; this ran as Service 870, and Premier's use of a separate number soon ceased. The service ran from Friday to Monday until the autumn, following the route of Services 77/78 from Clacton to Leicester before continuing through the Potteries to Chester and Liverpool. Glasgow Service 88 became a joint operation with Western SMT, running in both directions on Fridays and Sundays, with single fares now available from Scotland.

Two more new Reliances arrived in December, GER913/914N, bringing the number of grant coaches to eight. They began their lives on express services, although GER914N (a Service 5 performer) was initially allocated to Chrishall and made a few appearances on the stage routes into Cambridge. Services 1 and 9 had received a boost by being allowed to pick up and set down within the city boundary, although local passengers waiting in Trumpington and Newnham regarded the blue buses with a certain amount of suspicion to begin with. Despite this easing of restrictions, the reduced role of the buses continued to be apparent. The last full-time conductor at Chrishall had been made redundant in March, the seasonal Wednesday Service 16 (Sawston - Royston) ran for the last time in September and the first of the ex-Devon General Reliances (VDV800) was withdrawn in November. The local Royston journeys on Service 16 continued, but the withdrawal of another rural link was one more step towards a sad but inevitable event: on the last day of 1974, the inconveniently sited depot at Chrishall closed. Many light miles were being clocked up as empty vehicles made their way along remote country roads to reach the fitters, and a suitable site for a depot in Cambridge had at last been found. At the turn of the year, the new depot at Kilmaine Close, on the northern edge of the city, took over from the primitive premises inherited from Weeden's. The Traffic Department had already transferred to Cambridge, and in the last, cold days of December it was now the engineers' turn to move out. The move represented a major upheaval, as Chrishall depot provided valuable local employment for a number of villages, and several of the garage staff now had to travel into Cambridge to work. Some of them crewed the vehicles which were still outstationed for the remaining operations in the area. Initially two vehicles were parked at a farm near the old depot, with others at Barley, Duxford Aerodrome and Fowlmere. The depot was sold to Funston's, a local haulage contractor who later moved into full-sized coach operations, while the village continued to be served by infrequent buses to Cambridge (Service 9), Saffron Walden (Service 12) and Royston (Service 43). Late-night and Sunday buses had ceased by this time, and it all seemed a long way from the early post-war years, when the depot was a major junction for several bus routes and there were express services to London and Clacton.

The new premises at Kilmaine Close included a very well-equipped workshop, with four linked pits and an area for body repairs and repainting, stores, tyre department, steam-cleaning facilities, offices and a boardroom. There was no morning run-out as there had been at Chrishall. Buses began their day's work at Haverhill or at one of the rural outstations, while the express services were still largely staffed by drivers who were outstationed for the lucrative contract services. Much of the work of the traffic office was done by telephone, but most vehicles called at the new depot to refuel and wash down, although the site was not large, and parking was limited. For several years an additional parking area was in use at nearby Cowley Road (now used by the successful Cambridge Park & Ride service); this replaced the site at the old cattle market. As well as being within easy reach of both Drummer Street and the Pye factory, the new depot had facilities and equipment well-suited to the maintenance of the increasingly modern fleet. It did a great deal to make operations more efficient as well as improving the Company's image.

The bus network saw several welcome increases. From 20th January, the Saffron Walden town services were greatly increased, to the requirements of Essex County Council. Regular-frequency weekday services were now provided to several parts of the town, including Rowntree Way, Pleasant Valley, Holmer Cross and Whiteshot Way. The latter two points had once been reached by Service 15, but all buses on the new network ran as Service 14, regardless of terminus! Other changes saw the Saturday extension of Service 59 (Haverhill - Audley End Station) to provide one return journey into Saffron Walden from Clavering, Wicken and Arkesden. Adjustments were also made on the other services into Saffron Walden (11/12/29/38), although Service 12 disappeared completely soon afterwards. The last fragment of this once-lengthy route was replaced in June by an extension to the 43, restoring a through Royston - Chrishall - Saffron Walden service on certain days. Other withdrawn sections of route began to be reinstated. Following discussions with Hertfordshire County Council, the Royston - Barley section of Service 26 was revived, bringing back the Royston - Bishop's Stortford link on Thursdays and Saturdays. At the same time a new circular Service 27 was introduced from Royston to Brent Pelham on Wednesdays and Saturdays, which covered part of Service 26, and also served the village of Hare Street. Careful planning by the drivers ensured that the vehicles on Services 26 and 27 did not meet on the single-track road between Meesden and Brent Pelham on Saturdays!

The Saffron Walden town services were revised and increased in January 1975 to meet the requirements of Essex County Council. The new services provided far more buses than the previous ones, with regular all-day services to several parts of the town replacing the previous service, which only operated on three days a week apart from school journeys. This former Devon General bus was photographed emerging from Church Street. *C W Routh*

Although two of the ex-Devon General Reliances retained their cream roofs, later repaints of the type had the roofs painted electric blue, which was far less attractive. In this view at Drummer Street, VDV804 still looks very presentable despite 17 years service as it waits to depart on Service 9. *C W Routh*

The four AEC Reliances delivered in 1975 were the first of many with Plaxton bodywork. The new coaches were all to grant specification, and appeared on all types of operations, as shown in this 1981 view in Drummer Street. NEB348R (new in 1976) is working on Service 44 to Fulbourn, while JVE372P of the original batch has arrived on express Service 39 from Oxford, which continued to be worked jointly with Percival's Motors. *K Lane*

More coaches were needed for the summer traffic, and they broke new ground by having Plaxton bodies, the first such vehicles owned, apart from a solitary ex-Drayton's Bedford WTB. Due to pressure of work, the Alexander factory in Falkirk could not supply new bodies quickly enough, and their new T-type body would never appear in Premier Travel livery. (Interestingly, Eastern Counties switched to Alexander bodies for its 1975 deliveries, having previously specified Plaxton products). There were four new coaches (JVE370-373P), with Panorama-style bodies, which were far more coach-like in appearance than the Alexanders had been. The Plaxtons were to grant specification, but all four entered service on coach duties, working the usual mixture of express, private hire and excursions, as well as appearing on contract work (now exclusively performed by coaches). The bright new livery suited them well, the new logos and distinctive destination displays (with service numbers in blue) giving additional touches of individuality. They looked smart and modern and they further enhanced Premier's reputation as a progressive coach operator, but to many they were less distinctive than their Scottish-built predecessors. Alexander bodies were rare in the south, and the type had become an instantly-recognisable part of Premier Travel's operations. The Directors were obviously impressed with the new coaches, however, and ordered four more.

Several older vehicles were withdrawn, including the first of the 36-foot Harringtons (NMU6/7 and AMX9A). More ex-Devon General Reliances also reached the end of the road (VDV795/806), along with most of the double-deckers, although the surviving pair were, surprisingly, repainted in electric blue and cream and survived for two more years. The two-person crews needed for these buses had become an unaffordable luxury on a full-time basis, and by this time there was only one full-time crew left. Driver Roope and Conductor Lamb were normally to be found with 326NJO on the Haverhill town services (52/54/57), although they occasionally escaped onto Services 44, 55 and 56 to provide some variety. The other double-decker (318NJO) became a regular peak-hour performer on Service 9, although it worked other routes on Saturdays. It even put in a surprise appearance in the summer on new Service 27 (Royston - Brent Pelham circular). The crew were both part-timers, and an Ordnance Survey map was a useful item of their equipment until a few surprised passengers had been picked up to show them the way! This was also the last occasion when a double-decker appeared on Services 16 and 43.

The express network saw further changes, as holidaymakers continued to head for the sun abroad at the expense of traditional British resorts. The more popular summer services still ran from the end of May to the end of September and Great Yarmouth, Bournemouth and Clacton were still popular destinations, although the Worcester section of Service 71 did not reappear in 1975, the service now starting from Banbury. The overnight journeys on Services 5, 74/75 had also ceased by this stage, while Service 3 to Skegness now called only at St Ives between Cambridge and Spalding. Further cuts at the end of the season removed Services 37 (Haverhill - Great Yarmouth) and 73 (Bedford - Cromer) from the timetables.

On the other hand, Service 5 now ran daily throughout the year from Birmingham to Harwich, with daily services also operating on Services 38, 39, 77/78, 79 and 183. Holiday habits were changing, but long-distance interurban coach travel was becoming increasingly popular. The next few years would see these trends continue as the fleet became more standardised than ever before.

FLEET STANDARDISATION
1976-1980

Premier Travel celebrated its 40th anniversary in 1976, and over the next five years the company standardised on Plaxton-bodied AEC Reliances. Fleet updating took place rapidly, with all types of operations increasingly worked by the new vehicles. The one driver/one vehicle policy continued and, until the ending of the Bus Grant scheme in 1980, many of the new coaches began their lives on stage services. Some older passengers did not care for the high entrance steps, but the riding qualities of the new vehicles were much appreciated. On the other hand, enthusiasts mourned the disappearance of the varied and characterful fleet of earlier days and for them it would never be the same again, although the transformation was undeniably impressive.

Long-distance express traffic continued to increase, while the summer-only services declined further until few were left. Private hire and contracts remained important, and the special relationship with Pye continued. At the start of the year there were 27 Pye contracts, and at Haig Road the coaches now used a purpose-built coach station, with numbered departure bays, which replaced the earlier open parking area. The bus network remained remarkably static, although a few more expansions took place.

Four more Plaxton-bodied Reliances arrived in January. KVE906-909P had the new, more upright Supreme body, and were the first Plaxtons to enter service on stage routes. Several more Harringtons were withdrawn soon afterwards. Service changes in 1976 were few, although Service 40 (Bedford - Hunstanton) was extended to Cromer to replace the withdrawn Service 73. In Luton, services now called at the town's new bus station, while plans were being made for a new bus station in Haverhill. Premier was still the sole provider of local services in the town, and Service 52 was extended to run via new estates at Chilmswell and Hales Barn as well as Chalkstone.

A development which never came about concerned the old-established Burwell & District Motor Services, based in the village of that name, to the north of Cambridge. Always associated with Daimlers (though latterly an AEC user as well), the firm was run by members of the Mansfield family who now wished to retire. They were anxious that their business should remain independent, and discussions regarding a takeover took place with several local operators, including Premier Travel. Although the Burwell concern had some coach work, it was mainly a rural bus operator and it is perhaps not surprising that nothing came of the talks. The business actually passed to Eastern Counties in June 1979, leaving Premier Travel and Whippet Coaches as the only independents with stage routes into Cambridge.

Still more new Reliances (NEB346-349R) arrived in the autumn, and the last of the ex-Devon General buses were withdrawn (VDV794/797). Several of the ex-Barton coaches were also sold, and only two remained at the end of the year. A new travel agency was opened near Market Hill, in Rose Crescent, and several celebrations took place. Mr Lainson celebrated his 65th birthday and retired as Managing Director, his place being taken by Mr F N Matthews. To

The new coaches delivered in 1976 all had the new and more upright Plaxton Supreme style of body. Seen in Birmingham on a well-loaded relief journey in July 1984, this coach was still displaying Service 5 over a year after the service became a joint operation with National Express. Premier Travel retained the majority of operations of the service, with Midland Red providing the rest as Service 905, Premier adopting the National number soon afterwards. *K Lane*

mark the occasion Mr Lainson and Mr Matthews unveiled a foundation stone at Kilmaine Close which had been hidden from view since the depot opened, nearly two years earlier. It was Mr Lainson's 40th year with the company he founded in 1936, and a special dinner was held in his honour at the University Arms Hotel on December 22nd. It was very much a time for congratulations, for Mr Lainson was made an OBE in the New Year Honours List. As Chairman of the newly-styled Premier Travel Group he continued to take an active interest, as did Mrs Lainson, who had retired as a Director a few years earlier.

An era ended in 1977 with the withdrawal of the two AEC Bridgemasters, and the last full-time conductor was made redundant. For the first time since the early post-war years Premier had an all single-deck fleet, consisting entirely of AEC Reliances. Additional coaches were urgently needed, and five secondhand Plaxton-bodied Reliances were purchased, the first pre-owned coaches for three years. They came from various independents and were not fitted for one-man bus work. Another pair of new coaches also arrived, PCE601/602R bringing to fourteen the number of Plaxtons to grant specification.

The long-distance services increased steadily, with three daily journeys now operated on Service 39 (Cambridge - Oxford), while Liverpool Service 870 reached Clacton every day except Tuesdays and Wednesdays, when it terminated at Cambridge. The decline of the summer services continued, however, and the end of the season saw the disappearance of Service 81 (Haverhill - Minehead) and the Harwich - Bangor service (now numbered 587 in the National series). An application was also made for a Clacton - Sheffield service jointly with Yelloway and National Travel, following the opening of the Sheffield Interchange in September. Nearer to home, a less glamorous but still useful terminus came into use when the Market Hill stops in Haverhill were replaced by a spacious new bus station, which included a smart and modern Premier Travel Agency. Further updating was apparent when the next batch of new coaches began to appear; RVE650/651S arrived at the end of the year, with another four still on order.

The Sheffield service duly commenced, further extending the network. Service 355 was part of the new Sheffield Interchange, and was worked in conjunction with National Express (as it was now known) and Yelloway. Premier's participation was normally limited to providing relief vehicles, although it operated the service coaches at busy times. Some publicity material referred to this route as Service 92, but in practice coaches displayed the National number. The character of the express operations continued to change rapidly, and Service 38 was extended early in 1978 to provide a Sunday service to London from the old aerodrome at Stradishall, now High Point Prison. Premier Travel became the sole operator on the Heathrow Airport service, although this retained its National-style service number (079) for many years. From 1st May, local passengers were at last allowed on Service 39 between Cambridge and Hitchin.

Three weeks later coaches began to go much further afield when the Eastlander Continental started. Service 779 was jointly operated by the four partners in the pool (Premier Travel, Grey-Green, National and Tricentrol, as the Luton-based operator was now known), in association with Townsend-Thoresen. It followed the Service 183 route from Cheltenham to Felixstowe, and after an overnight crossing to Zeebrugge, the coach continued to Bruges and Brussels. It operated on three days of the week in each direction and ran until September. The established Eastlander services continued, by now extended at both ends to Walton-on-the-Naze and Gloucester.

Further joint operation began when Service 40 (Bedford - Cromer) was combined with existing services of York Brothers of Northampton. The new service ran either from Northampton and Wellingborough, or from Bedford and St Neots to Huntingdon, before continuing to Great Yarmouth. Yorks retained their old-established Northampton - Cambridge - Yarmouth service, and both operators benefited at a time when traditional holiday services were declining. Service 66 (Haverhill - Felixstowe) and the Birmingham - Southend service (latterly 599) disappeared at the end of the season. The original joint Yelloway services (74/75) were also withdrawn under these numbers, although Kettering and Huntingdon were still served by certain journeys on Services 77/78. The summer of 1978 also saw the main part Service 5 operating in sections (Birmingham to Clacton and Cambridge to Harwich), with a connection at Colchester for passengers from the Midlands travelling to Harwich. The Saturday Leicester - Clacton journeys continued, but it was the start of the decline of the Harwich section.

Fleet replacement had become even more rapid, and six more Plaxtons arrived during the year. RVE296/297S and RVE652/653S came in time for the summer traffic, and were later joined by WEB406/407T. The most notable withdrawal was that of AVE555B in June, the first of the Alexanders to go, although its twin (AVE444B) survived a little longer. Older, Harrington-bodied AMX8A also continued in service, despite withdrawal of newer Harringtons.

The balance of the order for Reliances (WEB408-411T) arrived early in 1979, bringing to 26 the number of AEC/Plaxton coaches delivered new. They replaced more Harringtons and Alexanders, including the 1965 pair (DCE800/801C). They were also significant in being the last AECs purchased. AEC was now part of British Leyland, and the Southall factory was to close. This was definitely a setback, for having standardised on new AECs for several years Premier Travel was unable to buy any more. The Chief Engineer (Mr Gifford) visited the factories of DAF and Volvo, and Duple-bodied Volvo demonstrator GHS7T was borrowed. However, Leyland was finally considered to be the best option in view of the readily-available back-up services, despite recent industrial troubles. It was decided to order ten Leyland Leopards, with a specification as close as possible to that of the newest Reliances, including manual gearboxes. Leyland also guaranteed future supplies of spares for the AECs. The decision to order Leopards was welcomed by Mr R Moore, who had recently joined the company. Very much a Leyland enthusiast, Mr Moore became Chief Engineer soon afterwards, when Mr Gifford retired.

Further co-operation between operators came when Service 9 (Cambridge - Chrishall - Great Chishill) had its timetable co-ordinated with that of Eastern Counties 103, which followed a similar route as far as Pampisford. The Service 9 journeys to Haverhill Road Corner in Stapleford were withdrawn, while Eastern Counties buses now ran via the water tower in Sawston. The housing estate had previously been solely Premier territory, and the larger operator wasted no time in erecting bus stop signs, a luxury the blue buses had managed without! The peak journeys from and to Great Chishill on Service 9 continued to be conductor-operated (using one of the older coaches), and Eastern Counties converted all of Service 103 back to crew operation on weekdays, with Bristol Lodekkas.

The new Leylands (BVA784-789V and CJE452-455V) had all arrived by April 1980, and were Premier's only Leopards. They were very similar in appearance to the last AECs, with standard Plaxton coachwork. They were also the last grant coaches, and several entered service on local stage routes. One of them (BVA789V) featured in the opening of the new Kings Cross Coach Station on May 14th, while BVA784V, with Driver C Malkin, came first in its class at the Southend Rally. The Leopards swept away no fewer than eight Alexanders, leaving only the eight bus-grant vehicles. Harrington bodies also disappeared, with the withdrawal of ex-Surrey Motors HLP10C.

There were few express changes before the autumn, although Eastlander Services 182/183 were renumbered 782/783 in May, and extra stops were introduced between Wheatley and Oxford on Service 39 in July. Big changes were imminent, as the Conservative government announced plans for coach deregulation. At the end of the season the remaining Midlands - Clacton summer services were withdrawn, comprising Services 67 (from Rugby), 71 (from Banbury) and 76 (from Kidderminster, regularly operated by Whittle's Coaches on hire). Joint Service 870 (Clacton - Liverpool) also disappeared, along with the Eastlander Continental (Service 779) after only two seasons. The fast Cambridge - Blackpool journeys on Services 77/78 ran via Rushden for the last time and Service 38 (Haverhill - London) was reduced to a Friday to Monday operation, with weekend extensions to Kedington and Stradishall. From September Service 5 became a daily all-year-round service from Birmingham to Clacton, no longer serving Harwich.

On the bus side interest was provided by the restoration in September of the Linton - Newmarket section of Service 46 (originally Saffron Walden - Newmarket), which had been withdrawn in 1957 after the Suez crisis. Following a survey in the area it was reinstated for a six-month trial period on behalf of Cambridgeshire County Council, and the Tuesday return journey was sufficiently well-used to justify its continuation. An extra journey was also introduced on Service 42 (Haverhill - Bumpsteads circular), and as a new era in coach travel dawned, Premier Travel's bus routes were proving that they still had a useful role to play.

THE AGE OF THE COACH
1980-1985

The Transport Act (1980) came into force on 6th October. It removed the need for road service licences on excursions and tours, and on express services where journeys of 30 miles or more were possible. Stage services were also redefined as services where passengers could be set down within 30 miles in a straight line from the picking-up point. These still needed individual licences, as did operators, vehicles and drivers.

Not surprisingly, a large number of operators started running competitive new express services. The most significant was the short-lived British Coachways, which began operations on the first day. It was a consortium of established coach operators, offering six new services from King's Cross with fares well below rail and National Express levels. Prominent among the operators involved was Grey-Green, which appeared on all the services. Several others later joined, including York Brothers. National Express quickly reduced its fares in order to compete with the new services.

British Coachways did not challenge any of Premier Travel's express services, which were essentially cross-country rather than inter-city, and after due consideration the Directors decided that Premier should continue to work with National Express, with whom there were already several joint routes. Co-ordination between between Premier and National services was also evident; for example, Service 5 connected at Cambridge with National 320 from Bradford and Leeds, giving a convenient Yorkshire - Cambridge - Essex facility. Connections at Birmingham for North Wales were also well-established, and the inclusion of Service 5 in the Birmingham Interchange made more connecting journeys possible, including one to and from Liverpool which offered a faster journey time than the former Service 870 had done.

From November 1980 two additional journeys were introduced on Service 5 from Friday to Monday, and with the start of the summer timetables, in May 1981, new stops were provided at Dunsmore Heath and Brafield-on-the-Green. The latter point was approximately 30 miles from Cambridge, and local fares were introduced on the Cambridge - Northampton section. As a result, United Counties diverted its Cambridge - Northampton bus routes (by now numbered 128/129) via Drummer Street, instead of Lensfield Road, in order to compete with the new facilities. The local fares were available on the joint Yelloway services, and these were also revised. New Service 70 offered a Friday to Monday summer service between Ipswich, Cambridge and Rochdale via Stafford, Newcastle-under-Lyme, Hanley and Altrincham. It covered parts of the old Service 870 as well as giving faster journey times from East Anglia to Manchester. Services 77/78 continued unchanged and still served the section via Huntingdon on summer Saturdays. The fast overnight Clacton - Blackpool continued on Fridays, while an even faster daytime journey to the Lancashire resort was offered by Service 76 on Saturdays. This was the motorway express service from Cambridge, calling only at Bedford, Northampton, Leicester, Loughborough and Preston, with a journey time of just over seven hours. Service 75 reappeared as the Saturday Leicester - Huntingdon - Clacton journey previously operated as part of Service 5. Other new coach facilities included additional stops at the Oxford end of Service 39, coaches now calling at Headley Way and Lathbury Road in Summertown (referred to in timetables as "North Oxford"). The Glasgow service now operated from Hemel Hempstead, with a feeder coach from Dunstable. Western SMT's presence as a joint operator led to the appearance of Premier Travel coaches showing both operators' service numbers, in this case 88/926.

Coaching developments were not confined to express services. Following deregulation, Young's Coaches of Rampton introduced a Cambridge City Tour, using an ex-Crosville Bristol Lodekka open-topper. Although this was unsuccessful, Young's then proposed an ambitious programme of excursions from Drummer Street. Meetings were immediately arranged between Premier Travel, Young's and Eastern Counties, and the outcome was a well-organised joint programme, with participation by all three operators. Known as Companion Tours and operating throughout the year, the new venture was a separate legal entity. An attractive brochure was produced and one Young's vehicle appeared in a special green and white Companion Tours livery. The name was the idea of Premier's Commercial Manager, Mr G Bray, who did a great deal over the years to break down the barriers which existed between rival operators. Mr Bray suggested the name after watching a television episode of 'The Good Companions' by J B Priestley. It was very appropriate for a programme of coach excursions: did not the great Yorkshireman himself embark on 'An English Journey' by motor-coach in the 1930s? Premier had always operated excursions, but latterly they formed a very small part of operations, and participation in Companion Tours greatly increased the revenue from this type of work.

Opposite Photographed when new, this coach was one of the ten Leylands delivered in 1980 which were notable in being Premier's only Leopards. They were also the last bus-grant vehicles and the last vehicles delivered in the two-tone blue livery. They were purchased after discussions with Leyland following the closure of the AEC factory, and their specification closely matched that of the newest Reliances. *R H G Simpson*

There had been another bus revival on 29th April, when a new Service 12 was introduced at the request of Cambridgeshire County Council. It restored part of Service 16, with one return journey on Wednesdays from Duxford village to Royston, calling additionally at Shepreth, Meldreth and Melbourn. No fleet additions were made in 1981, but a notable sale involved VER262L, the first of the bus-grant Alexanders to go. It went to Percivals of Oxford for contract work, and was later joined by VER261L. Both vehicles were subsequently re-registered.

Five impressive new coaches arrived in 1982, and VAV254-258X broke new ground in several ways. They had the new Leyland Tiger chassis, fitted with Plaxton Supreme V bodies, following the loan of demonstrator FRN801W with the same chassis/body combination. VAV257/258X appeared in the British Coach Rally at Brighton. The new Tigers were to a higher specification than previous coaches, with carpeting and soft trim, and all entered service on coaching duties. They also introduced a new livery of metallic silver and electric blue. Their seating capacities gave an indication of increased loadings: two of them could seat 55 passengers, and as many as 57 could be squeezed into VAV258X.

Withdrawals of the secondhand Plaxtons began, although long-distance coach travel was increasing rapidly and there were several more extensions. In April two additional journeys were introduced on Saturdays and Sundays on Service 079 (Cambridge - Heathrow Airport). More coaches were provided for air travellers in May, when Service 39 was diverted to serve Luton International Airport. Premier had briefly served the airport with Service 80 in 1964, and the new arrangements replaced the service of JR Deluxe Coaches of Foulden, Norfolk. (This short-lived new company, run by a former Premier driver, had no connection with the later J&R Tours of Teversham, Cambridge). On May 28th another service to Glasgow started in conjunction with Western SMT, this time from Cambridge, St Ives and Huntingdon. Different service numbers were again used by the two companies, and the operation was referred to as 'Services 89/927'. A spin-off from the Glasgow services was the regular use of Western SMT coaches on Premier's Services 3 and 34 to Skegness. Service 5 was also increased on May 28th, and now had two daily journeys between Cambridge and Birmingham, one of which originated in Clacton. Cambridge was also linked to Colchester and Clacton by a new Service 71, which started on June 20th. This ran via Bury St Edmunds and Ipswich, but it only lasted for one season.

The summer also saw the start of a series of rapid changes to Service 38 (Haverhill - London). This had seen few alterations since being acquired from Burgoin, although the Monday journeys had ceased in January and the midweek operations disappeared in 1980. Now a daily service was again offered, for this was also the age of the commuter coach, and Premier began to build up this type of traffic. An early coach was introduced from Haverhill via Horseheath and Linton to Saffron Walden. It then served additional stops in Newport and Quendon on the old London trunk road, formerly the A11 but renumbered as the B1383 when the M11 motorway opened. After calling at Stansted and Bishop's Stortford the coach used the motorway as far as Redbridge Station (for Central Line connections). City-bound commuters could also disembark at Aldgate, or Cannon Street, before the coach continued via the Embankment and Hyde Park Corner to Heathrow Airport. The commuter service avoided the traditional King's Cross terminus, but other Monday-

Saturday journeys still called there before continuing to Heathrow. At weekends, Service 38 followed its traditional route between Haverhill and Saffron Walden via Steeple Bumpstead and Radwinter, the Sunday service still terminating at King's Cross.

Service 71 (Cambridge - Ipswich - Clacton) ceased on 25th September, two days before Service 70 (Rochdale - Cambridge - Ipswich) was withdrawn for the winter. As a further indication of the good relations which now existed with Eastern Counties, a new joint Cambridge - Ipswich service was launched in a blaze of publicity. It was one of several limited-stop services then being introduced by the NBC operator under the 'Eastline' name, but it was the only one to be jointly operated. Service 792 ran daily and for much of its length used the A45 trunk road, now the A14, stopping only once in most towns and villages. Advance bookings were possible, but fares were usually paid on the coaches. Eastern Counties' contribution was provided by their Ipswich depot.

Other changes were made on the Cambridge stage routes. Services 9 and 44 adandoned their traditional Drummer Street stops in May, moving into nearby Emmanuel Street. This followed the linking of Eastern Counties 103/184 to produce cross-city routes 183 and 184, which continued to be co-ordinated with Service 9 between Cambridge and Pampisford. On Service 44, a generally half-hourly frequency was introduced as far as Fulbourn, following the withdrawal of Eastern Counties 191 along Cherry Hinton Road. Most of the 44 operated from Haverhill depot, and buses also now ran in service to and from the outer termini at Kedington and Withersfield. This eliminated a lot of light mileage, as well as providing additional Cambridge - Haverhill buses, although the journey via Kedington was rather a marathon. Loadings at the Cambridge ends of Services 9 and 44 remained satisfactory, but there were now fewer passengers further afield. The outer section of Service 9 was very quiet and, early in 1983, the midday bus to Chrishall and Great Chishill was cut back to Ickleton and replaced by an extension of Service 1 from Fowlmere on Wednesdays and Fridays. Not far away, there was a welcome development in July. New Service 28 followed the former Newton - London route of the same number between Barley and Hare Street, before continuing to Buntingford. It was operated for Herfordshire County Council, with one return journey on Mondays. Several other new services into Buntingford began at the same time, following the revival of local market there. A route from Reed End, initially provided by Richmond's Coaches, was later taken over by Premier and became Service 25.

The introduction of the 'Eastline' Service 792 in September 1982 provided evidence for the improved relations between Premier Travel and Eastern Counties, with both operators even using the same service number! Photographed at Bury St Edmunds on the first day are Plaxton-bodied Reliance PCE602R and Eastern Counties' Alexander-bodied Leopard MCL931P, the latter showing the unhelpful destination display frequently associated with Eastern Counties buses. Mr J A Matthews of Premier Travel stands on the extreme left, whith Mr J S Madgett of Eastern Counties on the right. *G R Mills*

The 1983 Leyland Tigers were the first coaches with Plaxton Paramount bodies and the first with three-track number blinds. They also introduced another new livery, with royal blue replacing the electric blue of the previous year's scheme; the lighter shade of blue did not stand out very well against the silver background. The coach was photographed in Oxford on National Service 747. This absorbed Service 39 in October 1984 with Premier and Percivals retaining a majority share and reaching still more new destinations, including Lowestoft, Bristol and Swindon. *R H G Simpson*

From 2nd January 1983, Eastline 792 was extended at both ends to give a through Peterborough - Cambridge - Felixstowe service. A few additional stops were introduced, while the opening of the new Queensgate Shopping Centre in Peterborough made the service very popular.

There were major developments on the coach side in 1983. From 8th March, the business of the old-established Percival's (Anglia) Coaches was acquired, although Premier Travel had managed operations for two months prior to the takeover. None of Percival's eight assorted coaches were added to stock, although one was used by Premier for three months. Percival's (Anglia) had previously been Percival's Motors (Cambridge) Ltd, Premier's original partner on the Oxford service. The firm now concentrated on private hire and contracts, having changed its name when ties with Percival's Motors (Oxford) Ltd were broken some years earlier. The takeover provided two additional school contracts and a large plot of land not far from Kilmaine Close. Premier announced their intention of developing the site (which included a house and several former farm buildings) as a centre of operations.

More new Leyland Tigers arrived in the spring, with new-style Plaxton Paramount coachwork; FAV564-567Y had well-appointed normal-height bodies with 53 seats (except 567 which was a 51-seater) while soon afterwards came GFL527-529Y, which had high-floor bodywork with TV/video, on-board refreshments, toilet facilities and 49 seats, which could be grouped round tables if required. The high-liners were regularly used on services operated for Page & Moy Travel to the south of France and Monaco. The new coaches introduced an improved livery, with royal blue replacing the electric blue of the previous year's scheme; the lighter shade did not show up sufficiently well against the silver background. It was decided to repaint the Leopards in the latest scheme, starting with CJE453V, although the AECs retained the two-tone blue livery.

There were many more coach changes in 1983. A new variation of Service 38 introduced a commuter service on the original route as far as Hempstead.

Following the introduction of joint working with National Express, Service 5 was numbered in the National series as Service 905. Premier Travel was reluctant to use the new number, and some coaches continued to display Service 5, while others showed '5/905' initially, as seen here on WEB411T on a Clacton journey. Beside it stands NEB347R bound for Birmingham showing the new number, while WEB407T effectively brings Drummer Street to a standstill. WEB411T was numerically the last AEC, and its front end was rebuilt following accident damage. *G R Mills*

The coach then travelled through Thaxted, Henham and Elsenham to Stansted. Here it met the other commuter coach, which had travelled via Linton and Saffron Walden. Both coaches then followed the same route, one terminating at the Embankment and the other continuing to Heathrow. The Thaxted route was unsuccessful, lasting only until September.

The summer timetables introduced daily coaches on an all-year round basis on Services 77/78 between Lancashire and Clacton. Service 70 (Rochdale - Ipswich) also became a daily operation, but this was to be its last season. September also saw the final operations on Service 75 (Leicester - Huntingdon - Clacton), as well as the overnight journeys on Services 77/78 and the section via Huntingdon. Service 79 continued to increase, with two daily journeys and an additional coach at weekends. A new service for air travellers appeared in the form of Service 37, which ran from Cambridge to Gatwick Airport and followed an unsuccessful operation by Millers of Foxton. At weekends the service used the M11 and M25 motorways, but the Monday-Friday coach ran via Central London, and included an interchange of passengers at Stansted with the early coaches on Service 38.

However, the biggest change affected Service 5. On 22nd May 1983, an event happened which would have been unthinkable not long before: Service 5 became a joint operation with National Express. Premier Travel retained the major share of operations, Midland Red providing the National contribution as Service 905. Three daily coaches were provided between Cambridge and Birmingham (one of them from Clacton), together with connections at Northampton and extra coaches on Fridays and Sundays which gave a two-hourly frequency. At the same time, Premier became a joint operator on National Express 929 (Birmingham - Oxford - Southampton - Bournemouth). Participation by National on Services 5/905 was very valuable, and Cambridge became increasingly important as an interchange point. Clacton was still a popular destination, but the closure of Butlin's holiday camp provided a further illustration of changing holiday habits.

A special high-floor coach arrived in October; A638OEG had the 1000th Tiger chassis to be built, and was handed over at a special ceremony at Kilmaine Close. Unsuccessful attempts had been made to obtain the registration A1000LT, although the coach was proudly lettered "Leyland TIGER No. 1000" across the windscreen. It was entered in the Nice coach rally where it created a very good impression, as well as winning an award. Despite the success of the Leylands, two Scania K112 demonstrators were inspected in September, these being Plaxton-bodied A112MVS and Van Hool-bodied A112NBM.

As new coach operations began, a long-established feature of express coaching came to an end on 22nd January 1984, when the Cheltenham interchange ended. Increased interchange facilities were provided at Bristol and Oxford and the Eastlander was reduced to the Ipswich - Oxford section of Service 783, the seasonal 782 from Walton and Clacton now having ceased. The Eastlander continued to operate on a daily, year-round basis, and Service 783 was still jointly worked by Premier, National and Grey-Green, the fourth member of the pool having changed its identity again to become Tourmaster Coaches of Dunstable. The Cheltenham changes also caused the withdrawal of National 647 (Norwich - Cambridge - Cheltenham). National Express had been establishing interchanges at various key locations for a number of years, and Cambridge was an obvious centre where several increasingly busy services met. A through Birmingham - Lowestoft journey was now introduced on Service 905, following the route of National 747 east of Cambridge. Premier reluctantly ceased to refer to the route as Service 5, and thereafter the National number appeared in timetables. Premier Travel's contribution to Service 929 (Birmingham - Bournemouth) ceased, but Premier (and Yelloway) coaches continued to appear on Service 355 (now Colchester - Sheffield). Another shared operation (but a far more local one) saw Premier Travel vehicles on the Cambridge Park & Ride service, a contract previously worked solely by Eastern Counties.

Expansion continued from 15th April when the number of daily journeys on Service 39 (Cambridge - Oxford) was increased from three to five, while the start of the summer timetables on May 20th saw more developments. Service 355 was extended to Huddersfield, and two faster Cambridge - Rochdale journeys were introduced daily on the joint Yelloway services. The new journeys operated as Service 879, replacing Service 70 and running non-stop on the Northampton to Leicester, Leicester to Derby and Manchester to Rochdale sections, giving faster journey times for longer-distance travellers. Services 77/78 had been renumbered 877/878 in January, and the fast Cambridge - Blackpool motorway journeys reappeared for the summer as Service 876. The services were listed as part of the National network, although they remained under the control of the two independents.

At the same time Service 37 (Cambridge - Gatwick Airport) was extended on summer Saturdays to Brighton, and when Service 34 to Skegness started in June it was extended to start from Luton for the first time. Both Glasgow services offered overnight journeys on Fridays and Saturdays and daytime journeys on Saturdays and Sundays, Service 88 running from Hemel Hempstead, Luton and Milton Keynes and Service 89 from Cambridge, St Neots and Bedford. The coaches met at Northampton and continued their northward journey together. Western SMT continued to refer to their share of the operations as Services 926/927.

Delivered in 1984 in fleet livery, this Leyland Tiger Highliner was originally used on a US Air Force contract. It was photographed two years later, soon after it had been repainted in National Express livery for Service 376 between Cambridge and Glasgow, where a coach with on-board toilet facilities was required. The vehicle also appeared regularly on Eastlander Service 783, which was extended in October 1984 to Bristol, Newport and Cardiff, following its cut-back to Oxford. This view, in Dunstable, shows the silver and blue 'Premier Travel Group' logo. *K Lane*

Leyland Tiger A638OEG took part in the Brighton Coach Rally in April, and another similar high-specification coach arrived in July. The new vehicle (A695JER) entered service on a daily contract, operated for the US Air Force.

The politicians were once again busy. The deregulation of express services was judged to have been a success, and July 1984 saw the publication of the White Paper 'Buses', with bus deregulation among its many radical proposals, along with the selling-off of the National Bus Company. In readiness for this, the larger NBC subsidiaries were divided into smaller units, and from 9th September Eastern Counties was split. The well-known name and the red livery were retained for the eastern half of the company. The western area, with operations from Cambridge, Ely, Newmarket and Peterborough, passed to Cambus Ltd. The new company initially adopted an insipid livery of Cambridge blue and cream, later much-improved by the addition of dark blue. Eastern Counties' express operations passed to Norwich-based Ambassador Travel Ltd, another new company which now became Premier's partner on Eastline 792.

As privatisation approached, National Express continued to increase its influence, and on 28th October, Service 39 was absorbed into National's existing Service 747 (Lowestoft - Bristol). This increasingly important cross-country service already ran between Cambridge and Oxford via Bedford and Northampton, with an agreement that local passengers would not be carried over this section. This restriction ceased, and four daily 747 journeys now followed the Service 39 roads between the University cities. The three routes now followed were:

747   Lowestoft - Cambridge - Luton - Oxford - Bristol (including
        former Service 39)
        or Lowestoft - Cambridge - Northampton - Oxford - Bristol,
        or Cambridge - Milton Keynes - Oxford - Cheltenham - Gloucester.

Most of the coaches were provided by Premier Travel and Percival's Motors (Oxford) Ltd, with National (Wessex) operating the others. Coaches no longer called at Cambridge railway station, which had been an important stop when Service 39 first replaced the trains in 1968. Another October alteration affected Eastlander 783. Having been cut back to Oxford in January, this was now extended to Bristol and Cardiff.

This official view shows the first MCW Metroliner when new at Madingley, near Cambridge. It was finished to a very high standard, including many features introduced on the Leyland Tiger Highliners. Following in the tradition of the 'County' Daimlers, it was officially named 'City of Cambridge' by the Mayor outside the Guildhall on 1st February 1985. Three more Metroliners followed, but the unreliability of these coaches led to their disposal after only three years service. *Courtesy M J Gifford*

The joint operation of Companion Tours ended in 1984, although Young's Coaches continue to use the name. Eastern Counties had pulled out a few years earlier, and Premier Travel once again offered its own excursion programme. During the summer, operations moved to the former Percival's (Anglia) premises in King's Hedges Road, and further high-specification coaches arrived which were very different from the company's existing vehicles. The Birmingham-based bodybuilder MCW was now producing complete vehicles, and following trials with demonstrator A543WOB Premier Travel became the first independent to take delivery of a Metroliner Hi-Liner. With a price tag of £85,800, the new coach appeared at the International Motor Show in Birmingham. It was finished to a very high standard, with 47 seats and many features introduced on the newest Tigers. Registered B192JVA after the show, it was formally named 'City of Cambridge' by the mayor on 1st February 1985. It was a beautiful vehicle to ride in and to drive, and plans were made for setting up an MCW dealership.

Three more similar vehicles (B244-246JVA) followed in the spring of 1985. These had 49 seats and demountable toilets, allowing conversion to 53-seaters, although they were rarely used as such. B244JVA was officially named 'City of Birmingham' by the mayor of that city on 10th May.

The five former DMS-class Leyland Fleetlines reintroduced double-deckers to the fleet after an absence of eight years. They were neatly converted to single-door layout by Ensign of Purfleet, who also fitted improved heating systems. They looked very smart when delivered, and each one carried different and attractive allover advertising for the holiday, tour and coach operations of the Premier Travel Group. KUC983P's MCW body advertises travel opportunities to China.

Following on from the Metroliners, some very different vehicles arrived in June, in the shape of five former London Transport DMS-class Leyland Fleetlines, reintroducing double-deckers after an interval of eight years. Two had MCW bodies (KUC983/989P), the others having virtually identical Park Royal bodywork (KJD24/58/116P). All had been converted to single-door layout and fitted with improved heating systems, and each one featured individual advertising for the the Premier Travel Group. The intention was to use them on stage and school services. The latter were now available to any member of the general public brave enough to travel on them, and the blinds of the double-deckers included displays for Services 60-69, the numbers initially allocated to the school routes. Unfortunately, the Fleetlines were not well-received by passengers accustomed to coaches, which offered a far more comfortable ride. After a short period (mainly on Service 44), the Fleetlines were confined to school contracts, also appearing on the Park & Ride service. Like the AEC Bridgemasters, they suffered problems with overhanging trees, and their appearance became increasingly \battle-scarred, while the semi-automatic gearboxes caused problems initially. Transmission problems were also an unfortunate feature of the Metroliners, which began to make regular trips back to the MCW factory. Leyland once again became the choice for new

The takeover of Young's of Rampton in January 1986 brought several non-standard vehicles into the fleet for a while. Most were quickly sold, the only full-sized coaches retained being two Bedford YMTs with Plaxton bodies equipped to carry disabled passengers. Both were resold soon afterwards, and the older of the two is seen here at Colchester, clearly showing its dual door layout. The centre door was equipped with a wheelchair lift. *G R Mills*

coaches, and an impressive all-Leyland Royal Tiger Doyen (C519KFL) arrived in July. It joined Tiger A695JER and one of the Metroliners on the US Air Force contracts, which linked London's airports with the aerodromes at Lakenheath, Mildenhall and Bentwaters. Comparisons between the three types were thus possible, although C519KFL remained unique in the fleet.

More Alexanders were withdrawn, while Monday to Friday Service 42 (Haverhill - Bumpsteads circular) disappeared from the bus timetables. On the coaching side, the Skegness routes were combined, with Service 3 running through from Cambridge to Skegness while Service 34 ran from Luton to Huntingdon, where passengers normally transferred onto the coach from Cambridge. A similar operation began on the Glasgow routes, with the main service linking Cambridge with Glasgow on Saturday and Sunday mornings, while a feeder coach ran from Hemel Hempstead to Northampton on Sundays, returning on Saturdays. Premier's entire contribution ran as Service 89 and operation was now joint with Scottish Citylink, which published a separate timetable for Service 927, with no mention of Premier Travel. The services ceased in this form at the end of September. Another withdrawal, but only for the winter period, was Service 783 (Ipswich - Cardiff), which previously ran all the year round and had been extended to Barry Island at weekends during the summer. Grey-Green's share of operations also came to an end. A small extension was made in November when Service 079 was extended to the new Terminal 4 at Heathrow Airport.

In the meantime one of Premier's long-standing express partners had seen dramatic changes. On 5th July 1985, control of the Yelloway business passed from the Allen family to Carlton PSV, although Services 876-879 continued to operate as before. Recent publicity had even used the traditional character of the operations in an attempt to attract passengers, extolling the virtues of "The QUIET COACH service - you will not find noisy music, radio, commentary or video...You may sit where you like, smoke or not as you wish, read or gaze out of the large panorama windows at the passing countryside". The Yelloway fleet immediately saw drastic changes; Carlton PSV were Neoplan dealers, and the newer coaches in the fleet were quickly replaced by exotic Skyliner double-deckers, although so far as is known none of these appeared on the services to East Anglia.

Notable vehicles taken over from Young's were these two Mercedes-Benz vehicles, with Reebur bodies incorporating 21 coach seats. Photographed at Premier Park, they were the first minicoaches owned and the first vehicles in the fleet with foreign-built chassis. They lasted until the autumn of 1987 with Premier, by which time the company had purchased three new 12-seaters with the same chassis/body combination. *G R Mills*

From 30th November, Premier Travel's operations were greatly expanded by the takeover of Young's Coaches of Rampton, formerly a partner in the joint Companion Tours programmes. After starting with a minibus in 1959, Mr E Young had become a respected coach operator, with numerous British and Continental tours, as well as contracts and private hire. Premier Travel managed operations for a month before the sale, and continued afterwards to use eighteen of Young's vehicles. Many were non-standard, with DAF, Dennis and Bedford coaches in stock, leading to appearances of exotic DAF/Jonckheere double-deckers on Service 905. It was soon decided to retain only nine vehicles, including two Bedford YMT coaches with wheelchair-equipped Plaxton bodies (SVA924S and AEG121Y), and two small Mercedes-Benz/Reebur coaches, which became the first foreign-built vehicles ever owned by Premier Travel (WAV122X and A132MFL). The other vehicles retained were five more ex-London Transport Fleetlines (OJD126R and OUC25/27/28/31R). These were used solely on school services and retained Young's grey and red livery, although the other vehices were repainted. The takeover gave Premier another ten school services, five requiring double-deckers. There were also five school contracts in the Huntingdon area operated for the US Air Force, and three Social Services minibus routes. The disposal of the rest of the Young's fleet left Premier short of vehicles, and long-term hires became a feature over the next few months. Operators who helped out included York Brothers (with 6 Ford coaches), Beeston's (3 Reliances and a former Grampian Atlantean), J&R Tours of Teversham (1 Bova Futura) and Cambus (various Ford Transits).

Cambus was one of many operators to have adopted minibuses, and the introduction of new minibus networks was now a feature of the bus scene. The controversial Transport Act of 1985 came into force on 30th October. Road Service Licences for stage services were to be abolished (except in London), and any operator could run services provided the statutory period of notice was given. Many established operators now saw high-frequency minibus routes as a way of safeguarding their interests against competitive new services. Changes were also proposed to the system of subsidising loss-making routes, and County Councils would in future put out socially-necessary services to competitive tender. Bus operators now had to prepare for the biggest shake-up in their industry since the passing of the Road Traffic Act of 1930.

BUS DEREGULATION
1986-1987

Premier Travel celebrated 50 years of operation in what was a very significant year for bus and coach operators, and in January 1986 the company was busily preparing for D-Day on 26th October. Commercial services had to be registered by 28th February, and new-style timetables were published for all the stage routes, with the company's anniversary logo prominently featured.

January saw the official withdrawal of Leyland Tiger VAV255X, which was seriously damaged by fire while working on Service 38 during the previous year, while the departure of XVE814L left only two Alexanders in the fleet. The various hired vehicles returned to their owners, and there was a large intake of new stock. Five more Plaxton-bodied Tigers arrived in March; of these, C328PEW was in fleet colours, while C329-332PEW were significant in being the first Premier Travel coaches in National Express livery. Originally confined to the fleets of NBC subsidiaries, the familiar white scheme was now appearing on other operators' vehicles. The new Tigers carried silver 'Premier Travel Group' logos to make their identity clear to discerning travellers, and they soon appeared on Services 747 and 905. The latter operation was renumbered 405 from 27th April, when several extra stops were introduced. Both services continued to offer numerous connections to and from Cambridge, Oxford, Bristol and Birmingham. Additional stops were also introduced on Service 879 (Cambridge - Rochdale), which was diverted via Stoke-on-Trent.

Other interesting new vehicles arrived. C325-327PEW were Mercedes-Benz L307D/Reebur 12-seaters, acquired mainly for the ex-Young's Social Services contracts. C333PEW was a Bedford YMPS with luxurious Plaxton 30-seat bodywork, complete with toilet compartment. It was the first Bedford purchased new since 1950, and was the smallest executive coach owned. Seven secondhand Tigers also appeared, including FWH37Y, previously in the Yelloway fleet. One of the acquired Tigers (A833PPP, ex-Armchair) soon received National livery, as did VAV254/256/257X from Premier's original batch. Other coaches were similarly repainted over the next few years, some later reappearing in fleet colours. Further interest was provided by two Duple-bodied coaches: A137RMJ had the Caribbean-style body, while B424CMC had the Laser variant. Very different was HHY186D, a Bristol FLF6G new to the Bristol Omnibus Company, but latterly with Nelson, of Wickford. Unfortunately for enthusiasts, this interesting bus was purchased solely for driver training, and it never appeared in passenger service; an additional handbrake lever mounted on the staircase would have made this rather difficult! It was the only half-cab vehicle ever to carry the silver and blue livery, with a red stripe to distinguish it as a training vehicle, and it looked extremely smart.

The build-up of traffic on services to and from London's airports can be judged from this February 1990 view at Stansted. Showing two different fleetname styles, the two leading coaches are both bound for Saffron Walden and Haverhill, with another Premier vehicle behind. By this stage there were six weekday coaches in each direction on Service 38 and eight daily coaches to and from Cambridge on Service 78, which also served Heathrow and Gatwick. *G R Mills*

After standardising on Plaxton-bodied coaches for many years, the Premier Travel fleet was becoming much more varied in the mid-1980s. Several secondhand Leyland Tigers were obtained in March 1986, including a pair with Duple bodywork. This one came from Frames Tours of London and had the 'Laser' style of body. It was photographed at the US Air Force base at Mildenhall in May 1988, a few months before it was sold.
G R Mills

The other Duple-bodied coach to join the fleet in March 1986 had the 'Caribbean' body style,and came from Cavalier of Hounslow. Photographed at Premier Park a year later, its window stickers show it to be ready for action on Service 879 to Rochdale. This vehicles was transferred to the Sampson's fleet at Hoddesdon after Premier became part of the AJS Group. *G R Mills*

107

Meanwhile, a significant change to bus and coach operations in Cambridge started on 6th April, when the old, much-maligned bus station at Drummer Street was closed for rebuilding. Argument had raged for years over the provision of a new station, while the existing one became increasingly shabby and hopelessly inadequate. Although the site had never been ideal, it was very conveniently sited in the city centre, and it was decided to redesign the station to make more efficient use of the space available. The stops for most of the express services were moved to the existing Bays 12-15 (now known as the 'express stands'), with local bus services banished for ten weeks to various temporary stops at New Square and Parkside while the rebuilding of the main part of the station took place.

April 1986 also saw the start of new timetables for the services which would be run on behalf of County Councils under the new tendering arrangements. For Hertfordshire County Council, Premier Travel now operated Services 10 (Bishop's Stortford - Arkesden circular), 16 (Royston Town Service), 25 (Reed End - Buntingford), 26 (Royston - Bishop's Stortford), 27 (Royston - Brent Pelham circular), 28 (Barley - Buntingford) and 43 (Royston - Chrishall circular), with the through Royston - Saffron Walden journeys now running as Service 42.

Subsidy payments and concessionary fares had already become very involved for services on the Cambs/Herts/Essex borders, and some support for the 10, 26, 42 and 43 was also received from Essex County Council, for whom Premier Travel also provided Services 11 (Duddenhoe End - Saffron Walden) and 29 (Linton - Saffron Walden). To complicate matters further, part of the 29 was also provided for Cambridgeshire County Council, for whom Premier also provided Service 46 (Linton - Newmarket). The well-known independent Hedingham Omnibuses took over on Services 14 (Saffron Walden Town Service) and 59 (Haverhill - Audley End Station). Hedingham also assumed responsibility for the local Haverhill - Saffron Walden journeys on Service 38, which now became Service 18.

Changes were also made to some of Premier's Cambridge routes, all of which had been registered as commercial operations. Service 2 still provided certain journeys between Royston and Cambridge on what was otherwise Cambus Service 146 (formerly 108, but renumbered early in NBC days). A fast Monday-Friday morning journey for commuters was introduced, running via the main road and stopping only in Harston and Trumpington. The return trip was made during the evening peak and the commuter journeys ran as Service 3. (The Cambridge - Skegness Service 3 ran as part of Service 34 when the summer services reappeared.) Services 1 and 2 were integrated, with Service 1 diverted at Fowlmere to serve Royston once again, while Service 2 now reached Royston via Barton and Haslingfield, buses operating from the latter village over the hill to Barrington along a previously unserved stretch of road. The revisions increased Premier's operations between Cambridge and Royston, although Cambus was still the main provider. Changes were also made to Service 9, with most journeys now running to Duxford Aerodrome after leaving Sawston. The service now ran onto the museum site and also served Heathfields, the former married quarters which were being sold off as private housing. After leaving the airfield, buses proceeded in a loop via Duxford village, Ickleton and Hinxton before returning to Sawston and Cambridge. The Great Chishill journeys on Service 9 continued to serve Pampisford and the original route.

The busiest route from Cambridge was Service 44, running basically every half-hour on the Cambridge - Fulbourn section, with occasional forays further afield. It traditionally operated in Fulbourn via Windmill Lane to the White Hart, but in April was altered to provide a loop via the Baker's Arms and the village centre (hitherto served only by Eastern Counties/Cambus), returning via the original route. This only applied to journeys which terminated in Fulbourn, the through buses to Balsham and beyond remaining unchanged. The revision led to a reduction in frequency, with buses now running every 45 minutes, and this was not popular with passengers, despite the increased scope of the service.

The Haverhill - London service was reorganised again. Service 38 ran at weekends following its original route from Haverhill through Steeple Bumpstead and Radwinter, with all journeys now terminating at King's Cross. The commuter journeys were renumbered as Services 37 and 39. Service 39 followed the 38 route to Bishop's Stortford and then ran through Central London to Heathrow and Gatwick Airports, while Service 37 ran via Linton and Central London to Heathrow. Still more adjustments followed in June, with 37 running once more to Gatwick and 39 terminating at Heathrow, while a daily service was once again provided on 38, which continued to Heathrow on Mondays to Fridays.

Changes were becoming ever more rapid, and the company introduced a whole host of new connections on the remaining summer services. These included odd journeys on the flourishing Heathrow Airport service, which lost its National-style number and became Service 79 once more. The full list of services was as follows, with * indicating new operations:

Service
4   Peterborough*- Huntingdon - Cambridge - Hemsby.
34   Huntingdon/Cambridge - Skegness (Including former Service 3).
40   Northampton/Ely*- Cambridge - Hunstanton - Cromer (Operated
       jointly with Yorks Travel).
72   Haverhill - Cambridge - Southampton - Bournemouth.
78   Bury St Edmunds*- Newmarket*- Cambridge - Heathrow - Gatwick -
       Brighton.
79   Wisbech*- March*- Chatteris*- Ely*- Cambridge - Heathrow -
       Gatwick.

Each service offered one return journey on Saturdays, from May to September. All called at Drummer Street, but a new feature was the operation of an interchange at Premier Park. This was the new identity of the former Percival's premises, which became fully operational as a depot in May, the name being chosen after suggestions were invited from the staff. The interchange was an ambitious idea, which sadly turned out to be a final fling for the summer services; most of them disappeared at the end of the season, although Yorks continued to run to Cromer for a couple more years. The fast Service 876 journeys (Cambridge - Blackpool) also ceased. There was now far less demand for summer holiday services as more and more holiday-makers headed for the airports. Three daily Cambridge - Heathrow - Gatwick journeys were now provided, with an additional Monday-Friday coach as far as Heathrow. The section of route via North London was withdrawn, coaches running direct via the M25 after leaving Stevenage.

Cambridge has retained its bus station and, after years of argument, the dilapidated terminus at Drummer Street was finally rebuilt in the summer of 1986. Passenger facilities have been further improved in the last few years, although the size of the site and the combined entrance/exit still lead to congestion at busy times. One of the final batch of AEC Reliances was photographed departing on Eastline Service 792. Behind is a Cambus VR on the traditional Peterborough service, wearing the rather insipid NBC-style livery originally adopted by Cambus in the run-up to privatisation. *P J Relf*

Daily, long-distance services continued to develop, and the revamped Glasgow service started at the end of April. Now Service 376, it offered many new direct links on a daily basis, running via Peterborough, Doncaster, Middlesbrough, Newcastle and Carlisle. Operations were shared between Premier Travel, National Express and Scottish Citylink. Leyland Tiger A695JER was repainted into National Express livery for Service 376, as a coach with on-board toilet facilities was needed. It also operated on Eastlander 783 (Ipswich - Cardiff - Barry Island), which reappeared following its much-criticised winter suspension, jointly operated by Premier, National and Tourmaster.

On 22nd June, Drummer Street reopened. The redevelopment had included the removal of the central island, along with two large trees and Premier Travel's booking office. The latter was probably the least glamorous part of the Premier Travel Agency empire, and over the years it had expanded to take over part of the passenger shelter. In the meantime buses and coaches had become larger than they were in 1925 when the station was first used, and manoeuvring round the island had become increasingly difficult. Vehicles sometimes gained dents, or lost mirrors, as they jostled for position in the fume-laden atmosphere, while passengers battled their way through the chaos to get on board and escape from it all. Summer Saturdays were particularly difficult for drivers, passengers and inspectors alike, and jams in Drummer Street frequently led to long queues of traffic in the nearby streets. Removal of the island destroyed a small part of Premier Travel history, but it made vehicle movements a little easier.

Cambus previously had their own office across the road from Premier's, but new joint premises now opened as the Cambridge Travel Centre, initially in a large Portakabin, next to Bay 1. The new station was visually a vast improvement on the old, with eleven bus bays and much-improved shelters. Outgoing buses now reversed off the bays, avoiding incoming vehicles and the railings of Emmanuel College opposite. A dip was provided to warn unwary drivers that they were about to damage University property, but this did not stop a London-bound Green Line coach from collecting a bicycle on its rear bumper during the first few days. Premier Travel's Services 1, 2 and 3 used Bay 9, while Eastline 792 called at Bay 3 on its way north and Bay 6 when heading south. Services 9 and 44 continued to use the Emmanuel Street stops.

As bus deregulation approached, ticket interavailability between Services 1/2/3 and Cambus 146 ended; co-operation of this sort was now officially frowned upon, and joint working was deemed to be uncompetitive. Premier's ticket system began to change again, with the appearance of the first Almex machine. This was successful, and more were obtained to replace the Setrights.

Premier was also giving thought to future new vehicles. The unreliability of the Metroliners was a great disappointment and the coaches still made regular trips to MCW for faults to be rectified, with Metroliner demonstrator ABM399A loaned to provide cover. August saw the arrival of the first of many Volvo coaches (D524LCS), which had a Plaxton 53-seat body on Volvo B10M-61 chassis. Other demonstrators examined in the autumn were Scania D112MKX and Setra D620WPJ, along with a Van Hool/Acron and two DAF coaches.

Bus deregulation on 26th October saw no outward changes. The joint agreement with Cambus ended, but both operators continued to appear on Service 792. Having inherited Ambassador Travel's share of the service, Cambus produced the timetable, which now stated that "journeys operated by Premier Travel are shown for passengers' guidance only". It had always been assumed that this was the whole point of publishing timetables in the first place, but it emphasised the 'arm's-length' relations which were now expected to exist between operators. From 1st November, the Ipswich - Felixstowe section of the route was withdrawn, and a few weeks later Cambus left the shrinking National Bus Company and joined the private sector. It retained most of its traditional operations from Cambridge, although the new tendering arrangements introduced Miller Brothers of Foxton onto local bus routes. Initially operating on Service 197, Millers later gained other tenders and began commercial operations, leading to a long-running battle with Cambus.

Premier had been examining its commercial bus operations from Cambridge, and further revisions were made in April 1987. Service 44 was diverted at Cherry Hinton to reach new housing at Cherry Orchard, with all journeys additionally running through the grounds of Fulbourn Hospital, instead of calling only at the main gate. The half-hourly frequency was restored between Cambridge and Fulbourn, where two-way working was introduced round the loop. Clockwise journeys ran outwards via the Baker's Arms and returned via Windmill Lane, and these now ran as Service 45, although this number was not always to be found on the blinds of the older coaches and its use was later dropped. The number 44 was used for anti-clockwise workings and all through journeys; the latter still avoided the village centre. Following the success of the Royston commuter service, similar fast journeys were introduced from Haverhill on the 44. On Service 9, the section beyond Ickleton to Chrishall and Great Chishill was transferred to Service 1.

A complete break with tradition came in March 1987 with the purchase of ten Volvo coaches with Van Hool bodywork, the first wholly foreign-built vehicles in the fleet. This coach additionally had a wheelchair lift for the carriage of disabled passengers, and was one of two entered for the 1987 Coach Rally. It clearly shows its dual-door layout in this view at Madeira Drive, Brighton. *G R Mills*

March saw the arrival of ten new coaches. Following the successful operation of D524LCS, they had Volvo B10M-61 chassis, and with Van Hool coachwork they were Premier's first vehicles with foreign-built bodies. The new coaches were D342-345/350/351KVE and D846-849KVE. The registrations of 846-849 were chosen to avoid confusion with NEB346-349R, as coaches were referred to by the numbers in their registrations. Vehicles 846-849 were toilet-equipped 49-seaters, 350 had a wheelchair lift for disabled passengers while the others were 53-seaters. Premier's livery suited them very well, and two appeared at the Brighton Coach Rally.

Still more coaches were provided to the airports from 26th April, with six daily journeys on Service 79. Three of these ran direct from Cambridge to Stansted, Heathrow and Gatwick, the others calling additionally at Melbourn, Royston and Baldock, but omitting Stansted. Summer Saturday Services 4 and 72 reappeared on 23rd May, with Service 72 additionally serving Heathrow Airport. Although the other summer holiday services had ceased, day-trips to the coast were still popular, and new Sunday Service 22 (Cambridge - Hunstanton) started in June, continuing until the end of August. It competed with long-established Eastern Counties/Cambus operations, and Premier followed tradition by using a double-decker, passengers paying on board.

Significant withdrawals during 1987 saw off GER913/914N, the last of the once-familiar Alexanders, with GER914N retained for possible preservation. Most of the ex-Young's vehicles also departed, and by the autumn only the two Bedfords remained. The double-deckers went to Yelloway, now mainly a bus operator. It was very much the end of an era, for joint Services 877-879 between Clacton, Cambridge and Lancashire ran for the last time on 31st October, while another long-standing partnership ended when Percival's Motors (Oxford) Ltd ceased trading. National Express 355 (Harwich - Cambridge - Bradford) and 783 (latterly Felixstowe - Oxford - Cardiff) were also withdrawn, and a revised network was introduced from 1st November. The new services were:

Service
351   Burnley/Blackpool/Whitehaven - Manchester - Sheffield - Nottingham - Cambridge - Norwich - Great Yarmouth.
352   Rochdale - Manchester - Stoke-on-Trent - Derby - Leicester - Cambridge - Ipswich - Harwich.
405   Birmingham - Coventry - Cambridge the *either* Haverhill - Colchester - Clacton *or* Stansted Airport - Chelmsford - Southend.
747   Bristol - Swindon/Gloucester - Oxford - Luton - Cambridge, then *either* Haverhill - Colchester - Clacton *or* Norwich - Great Yarmouth - Lowestoft.

By this time, Service 79 and the Haverhill - London routes were the only express operations worked exclusively by Premier Travel on a daily basis. National Express assumed responsibility for the other express services, with Premier now providing coaches under contract. The complex joint-working arrangements ended, along with much of the administrative work which was previously necessary. Premier Travel operated thirteen diagrams on the new network, while Yelloway retained two return journeys on Services 351/352. Many new links were introduced, although Haverhill lost its direct coaches to the Midlands and the north. All 747 journeys now followed the former Premier/Percivals route through Luton, the Bedford variations having ceased in April. Another notable feature was the restoration of the Birmingham - Cambridge - Southend link on the 405, recalling the former joint service with Midland Red which ceased in 1979.

Premier's healthy performance was readily apparent, and ten more Volvo coaches were ordered. The company had come a long way, and had a modern fleet of vehicles, most of which had been purchased new. The annual turnover of the Premier Travel Group was now £28 million, and profits for 1987 were expected to reach a record high. However, Premier Travel Services Ltd (the bus and coach side of the business) only accounted for 11 per cent of this, and on 1st December 1987 came a dramatic statement. It was announced that Mr Lainson, together with Mr F N Matthews and his brother Mr J A Matthews (who had joined the company in 1969), wished to sell their holdings. Various negotiations took place for the sale of the entire Premier Travel Group, but in the event it passed to two other Premier Travel Directors, Mr P S Andrews and Mr R L Sargent. They wished to concentrate on the highly-successful Premier Travel Agency Ltd, Premier Airlines Ltd and Premier Holidays Ltd, and it was decided to dispose of Premier Travel Services.

The most likely bidder was Cambus Holdings Ltd. "Cambus Buys Premier Coaches" proclaimed the Cambridge Evening News, adding that the sale would take effect from 1st January 1988. The news was received with shock and resentment by the road staff, some of whom had previously worked for Eastern Counties, or Cambus, and did not wish to return. A group of drivers and traffic staff accordingly began determined efforts to drum up financial support from elsewhere, and at the eleventh hour (on 31st December 1987), a rival bid was accepted, financed by the West Yorkshire Road Car Co Ltd. This company had recently been purchased by Mr Alan Stephenson (Managing Director of East Yorkshire), and the bus and coach operations of the Premier Travel Group now joined those of West Yorkshire as part of AJS Holdings Ltd.

CHAPTER TWELVE

THE AJS ERA, WAR & PEACE, NEW BEGINNINGS

1988-1990

The negotiations for the AJS takeover were long and complex, and were not finally completed until 30th June 1988. One change which took place immediately was the adoption of an attractive new logo, for although the company could still use Premier Travel as a fleetname, the double-arrow symbol was now the property of the travel company. The new device revived the earlier use of King's College Chapel, with CAMBRIDGE on a banner below, and it soon became familiar on vehicles and publicity along with PREMIER TRAVEL SERVICES. Another early change was the branding of all stage services, however short, as local *coach* services, with the slogan "Travel in style with your local Coach Operator" on timetable leaflets.

Despite the seasonal destination display, Premier Travel's staff were facing an uncertain future when Van Hool-bodied Volvo D344KVE was photographed on 7th December 1987. The circular logo was replaced after the AJS takeover by one depicting King's College Chapel, while vehicles later displayed just 'Premier' as the fleetname. *G R Mills*

Premier's Managing Director was now Mr Ian Roberts, a former National man, who was largely responsible for setting up the Sheffield Interchange in 1978. Mr Roberts and his staff optimistically looked forward to further developments as part of a large bus and coach operating group. The silver and blue logo was prominently featured on the new bus stop signs which rapidly appeared all over the company's area, for a show of strength was now necessary. The management of Cambus resented the fact that their bid had been rejected, and hostilities between the two operators began. Cambus registered new minibus services in Haverhill and Royston, and extended their existing Cambridge - Teversham route to Fulbourn. In retaliation, Premier registered its own minibus networks to replace existing town services in Royston and Haverhill. Various alterations to the existing network also saw the start of two other new routes. By 29th February, the following developments had taken place:

Service
1   Amended to operate Cambridge - Hauxton - Fowlmere, extended
        peaks to Gt Chishill & Barley. Fowlmere - Royston section withdrawn.
2   Amended to operate Cambridge - Haslingfield - Royston/Harston
        (Mon-Sat).
3   (Royston - Cambridge Commuter Service). Extra stops at Melbourn
        and Foxton Station.
9   Sunday service Cambridge - Duxford Museum direct, extended to
        Royston on Special Flying Days.
16   (Royston Town Service) Completely reorganised and converted to
        minibus operation. From Town Centre to Hawthorn Way, Beldam
        Avenue, Coombelands, Burns Road (Mon-Sat).
22   New: Cambridge - Four Went Ways - Gt Chesterford - Saffron Walden
        (Mon-Sat, extended to and from Chrishall Wed).
40   New number for Service 44 Commuter Service Haverhill - Cambridge
        (Mon-Sat)
49   New: Cambridge - Cherry Orchard (Teasel Way). Services 44/45/49
        every 15 minutes on this section.
49   Existing service (Balsham - Haverhill) renumbered Service 59.
52/54/57 (Haverhill Town Services) Completely reorganised into
        Services 51/52/53/54/57 and converted to minibus operation. From
        Bus Station to Hales Barn (51),Chilmswell/Arrendene (52), Coupals
        (53), Chalkstone/Wilsey (54), Parkway/Clements (57). (Mon-Sat).
55   (Haverhill - Bury St Edmunds, Wed/Sat). Section via The Thurlows
        withdrawn. Extra stops at Denston and Horringer.
59   See Service 49.
136   Haverhill - Castle Camps - Shudy Camps - Bartlow - Linton (Mon-Sat).
137   As Service 136 and extended to Cambridge (Mon-Fri).

All except Services 55 and 59 competed with Cambus routes, Service 55 operating in competition with Eastern Counties. The journeys on Service 1 beyond Fowlmere were still crew-operated on Mondays to Fridays, by members of the garage staff. The extension to Barley was appreciated by the conductor (who lived there), and it also restored a link severed by the withdrawal of Service 27 in 1970. Services 136/137 covered former Cambus 136 and were operated for Cambridgeshire County Council.

Competition was fast and furious, with each operator determined to gain the upper hand. Six new minibuses arrived, E352-357NEG having Iveco 49.10 chassis and Robin Hood bodies with coach-style seating for 19 passengers. They entered service on 1st April, and replaced the minibuses previously on loan. East Yorkshire had provided Robin Hood-bodied Ivecos D44/54OKH, while Berks Bucks sent Carlyle-bodied Transits D827/828/831UTF. Bedford executive coach C333PEW was used as a back-up, and Iveco demonstrator D274SMA also appeared. Two of the Ivecos went into battle at Royston and three to Haverhill, competing with Ford Transits of Cambus. The blinds included displays for other Cambus destinations such as North Arbury, indicating that further battles were possible. Amidst all the conflict, Premier's journeys on Eastline 792 continued to appear in the Cambus timetable!

An interesting new coach purchased in the spring of 1986 was this Bedford YMPS with a high-specification 30-seat Plaxton body, complete with toilet compartment. Despite the destination display it did not appear on National Express 747 to Lowestoft, although it was used as a back-up vehicle during the short-lived minibus operations. *G R Mills*

Still with its metallic finish, one of the 1988 batch of new coaches sparkles in the sun a few months after entering service as it prepares to take up service on the ever-popular Service 79 from Cambridge to Gatwick Airport. These vehicles reintroduced Plaxton bodies to the fleet, again on Volvo chassis. Five of the ten were the last new coaches to arrive in fleet livery. They were also the last vehicles delivered before grey replaced silver as the main colour. *G R Mills*

Leyland Tiger/Plaxton C331PEW was withdrawn in March after being destroyed by fire in Bristol. As competing vehicles chased passengers on the bus routes, the new Volvo coaches arrived, and they saw a return to Plaxton bodywork. In April came E358-362NEG, in National Express livery, followed in May by E363-367NEG, in fleet colours. The latter appeared on the increasingly busy Service 79, now with eight daily journeys between Cambridge and the airports. National Express joined the private sector on 17th March, and from 1st May made a number of adjustments to its routes. Service 405 had been renumbered 305 and withdrawn east of Colchester on 31st January. The Cambridge to Colchester section was now transferred to Service 747 and extended again to Clacton. Revisions were also made to the terminal points of Services 351/352, including the diversion of the 352 to Blackpool, instead of Rochdale, and the replacement of the Burnley portion of the 351 by a new 381 (Blackpool - Burnley - Bradford - Leeds - Cambridge), operated by Cambus. The loss of the Rochdale section severed another link with Yelloway, while the changes also meant that day-trips to Clacton were no longer possible, the solitary Clacton journey on the 747 leaving Cambridge in the afternoon. From 1st May Premier Travel therefore introduced a daily summer journey from Cambridge over the old route to Clacton, and this ran as . . . Service 5! The Peterborough extension of Service 4 disappeared, the route reverting to its traditional Huntingdon - Hemsby form, while an increased Service 72 appeared. This offered a daily service from Cambridge to Heathrow via Royston and Stevenage, continuing to Bournemouth on Saturdays and Sundays, with the Saturday service from Haverhill as usual.

As signs of the new management became apparent, the fleet was once again becoming more standardised. The company was now primarily concerned with express, stage and contract operations, and high-floor executive coaches were no longer felt to be appropriate. Apart from the high initial cost, they did not fit in with the policy of transferring older coaches to stage work. Withdrawals began with the unreliable Metroliners, all of which joined the East Kent fleet and were later re-registered. Leyland Tiger/Plaxton Highliner GFL528Y was also sold, as were most of the double-deckers, although the solitary survivor (KJD116P) remained in regular use on a former Young's contract from Somersham to Kimbolton School. The two ex-Young's Bedfords departed, along with KVE906-909P (the first bus-grant Plaxtons to go), and Bristol FLF6G trainer HHY186D.

This Bristol FLF6G was the only half-cab vehicle to wear the silver and blue livery, modified by the addition of red stripes. It was new in 1966 to the Bristol Omnibus Company, and operated for Nelson of Wickford before being purchased by Premier Travel in 1986 for driver training duties. The bus was never used in passenger service and saw little use for training. It was sold two years later for further non-PSV use.
G R Mills

Meanwhile, loans to and from other AJS fleets continued. Two Plaxton-bodied Leopard coaches were borrowed from West Yorkshire (BWY664T and GWU562T), while Tigers A695JER and B424CMC were dispatched to East Yorkshire for six months.

Relations with Cambus had started to improve, and evidence for this was provided on 15th May when the Haverhill - London services saw yet more revisions. Service 38 (Haverhill - King's Cross, Fri/Sat/Sun) was renumbered 738, jointly operated by Premier Travel, Cambus and Green Line. The Green Line contribution was provided by London Country (North East) which had also recently joined the AJS Group. The new daily service followed the 38 to Woodford, continuing via Tottenham Hale and King's Cross to the traditional Green Line stops at Eccleston Bridge, Victoria. It partly replaced the withdrawn Cambus/Green Line 799 (Cambridge - Saffron Walden - Victoria), and its introduction provided more coaches than ever before between Haverhill, Saffron Walden and London, with a two-hourly frequency on weekdays. The first coach left Haverhill at 0630 and provided facilities for commuters, replacing Service 39. Commuters from the Linton area were catered for by Service 739 (Linton - Saffron Walden - Hyde Park Corner); this was a Monday to Friday operation by Premier Travel only, which covered the former Service 37.

Ever aware of the need to publicise itself, the company introduced another new logo in August. The word PREMIER now appeared in a more traditional style, and King's College Chapel continued to be featured, with PREMIER TRAVEL SERVICES surounding it and CAMBRIDGE below. The new device soon became widespread on coaches, timetables and bus stops.

The bus war came to an end, neither side having gained financially. Cambus withdrew their minibuses from Fulbourn and Royston, Service 49 (Cambridge - Cherry Orchard) ceased in June, and Premier reduced its minibus operations. The sections of Service 16 to Beldam Avenue and Green Drift were discontinued in Royston, while in Haverhill Premier's services were renumbered and reduced to Services H2 (Chalkstone and Wilsey) and H3 (Arrendene, Hales Barn & Coupals), the other sections being left to Cambus. The changes were very short-lived, as Premier withdrew all its remaining town services in the autumn, the Iveco minibuses passing to London Country (North East). Royston was thereafter served by the minibuses of Richmond's of Barley on contract to Hertfordshire County Council. Premier made a few other changes in the Royston area; the successful Cambridge commuter journeys on Service 3 were given the name City Express, while Service 12 (Duxford - Royston) was extended to start from Sawston, restoring another link which disappeared in the 1970s.

In Haverhill, Cambus now provided local operations along with Neal's of Chippenham, the latter on contract to Suffolk County Council. Premier's presence was now less obvious in the area, and apart from the withdrawal of the town services (which the company had started in 1960) two other significant events took place. First came the closure and sale of the former Burgoin depot in Camps Road, the vehicles initially moving to an outstation site on the industrial estate. Shortly afterwards (at the end of October) National Express withdrew the section of Service 747 which passed through the town. Colchester and Clacton could still be reached from Cambridge by the 351 route via Ipswich, but the withdrawal of the 747 journey (and also of Premier's summer Service 5) left the Cambridge - Halstead - Colchester section

The bus war with Cambus lasted only for a few months, and neither company gained financially. Two of the battle zones were the town networks at Haverhill and Royston, where Cambus registered minibus services early in 1988 to compete with Premier's traditional operations. Six of these Iveco 49.10 minicoaches with Robin Hood bodies were briefly owned, and this one is seen at Haverhill on Service 54. Hostilities had ceased by the autumn, when Premier withdrew all its remaining town services, and the vehicles all passed to London Country (North East). *G R Mills*

unserved by express coaches, a state of affairs which would have been unthinkable in the hectic days of Service 5 and the joint Yelloway routes. A further reminder of those busy days came at the end of November, for Yelloway had not been successful as a bus operator and, following the loss of several tenders, its remaining services were transferred to Crosville. It was a sad end for a once-great company. Although Service 747 lost its Clacton section, the route was extended at its western end, with the introduction of a daily through journey from Cambridge to Exeter, Torquay and Paignton. Another change saw Burnley served by Service 352, with the 381 diverted to Lincoln instead of Peterborough and Cambridge. A few other revisions were made to the services, and the start of the winter timetables saw Premier Travel providing twelve diagrams in the network. Fourteen coaches were now in National livery for Services 305, 351, 352 and 747.

January 1989 saw another livery change for Premier's coaches. The surviving AEC Reliances still carried the earlier two-tone blue livery, and it was now decided that at least some of them would be retained for the foreseeable future. Accordingly, RVE652S appeared in a new scheme of grey and blue. The effect was smart and attractive, and other repaints followed in due course. The new livery was not confined to the AECs, and grey replaced silver on newer coaches, the new colour being easier to retouch when minor body repairs were necessary.

There were also changes within the AJS Group. The troubled London Country (North East) company was split into two parts, known as County Bus & Coach and Sovereign Bus & Coach. These were initially trading names only, but in June they became separate companies, with their own operators' licences. Together with Premier Travel Services, they came under the control of a new holding company, London Country Travel Group, based in Hertford. Further reorganisation in September brought these companies under the control of the South of England Travel Group.

The new year saw a few changes to the commercial bus services. The Chrishall journey on Service 22 was withdrawn, and the route was extended in Saffron Walden to run in a loop via the estates at Rowntree Way and Ross Close. As well as providing a direct service to Cambridge, this brought Premier's coaches back to roads they had not served since April 1986, when Hedingham Omnibuses took over on Service 14. The end of January saw the diversion of Service 2 to serve Harston once again, with some journeys continuing to Fowlmere. The long-established Royston - Cambridge link was maintained by City Express Service 3, now operating non-stop on Mondays-Fridays, although it also served Melbourn, Foxton and Harston on Saturdays.

A more dramatic change affected Service 738. From 29th January Cambus and Green Line withdrew, leaving Premier Travel in sole charge once more. The service number reverted to 38, and the two-hourly frequency was maintained. The early commuter coach from Linton was re-routed via Haverhill, and Service 739 via Hadstock was withdrawn.

Premier Travel and Cambus had continued to operate Service 792 (Peterborough - Ipswich). This was renumbered X2, with the Bury St Edmunds - Ipswich section withdrawn on weekdays, and the Sunday service withdrawn completely. Further evidence of the improved relationship between the two was provided when a joint programme of excursions and tours was advertised.

Although vehicles were frequently transferred amongst the AJS fleets, the only such coach to be repainted in Premier Travel livery was this Plaxton-bodied Leyland Leopard from West Yorkshire, which arrived in April 1989. It followed the loan of two similar coaches during the previous year, and it was photographed a few months later leaving Drummer Street on the newly-styled Service X2. 'Speedline' was the new brand name for the former Eastline 792 which was still run in conjunction with Cambus, although the Bury St Edmunds-Ipswich section was withdrawn. Visible in the background is a Whippet Coaches Metro-Scania. *G R Mills*

Premier's inclusion in the AJS Group became increasingly apparent with the use of Premier Park for the storage of withdrawn County and Sovereign vehicles. Following the loans of the previous year, a further Plaxton-bodied Leopard (KUB546V) joined the fleet in April from West Yorkshire, and in May several similar coaches, which County had borrowed from Southdown, were loaned in turn to Premier. Most remained only for a few weeks, although one (OUF64W) stayed longer. Further executive coaches were sold, including the solitary Leyland Royal Tiger (C519KFL) and the little Bedford (C333PEW). Two of the Mercedes 12-seaters also departed, following the termination of the contracts they worked.

Changes were made on 15th April to the Hertfordshire County Council tendered services. These saw the company's reappearance on stage routes from Sandon to Royston, and from Royston to Hitchin. Both sections were once part of the lengthy Service 12 (Saffron Walden - Hitchin), which withered during the 1960s and finally died in 1975. The loss of the ex-Weeden's Service 10 (Arkesden - Bishop's Stortford) was made up for by new Service 17, which covered roads once served by London Country 386. Other new services were numbered 34 (this had a very short life) and 41, while Service 25 was extended to start from Reed instead of Reed End. The new services were:

Service
17   Bishop's Stortford - Wellpond Green - Puckeridge (Sat).
23   Royston - Therfield - Kelshall - Sandon - Rushden - Baldock - Letchworth - Hitchin (Tue), Buntingford - Chipping - Buckland - Sandon - Rushden - Baldock - Letchworth - Hitchin (Sat).
24   Sandon - Therfield - Reed - Royston (Wed/Sat).
34   Buntingford - Chipping - Buckland - Reed - Royston (Wed/Sat).
41   Royston - Reed - Barkway - Barley - Gt Chishill - Chrishall - Elmdon - Cambridge (Fri).

Another new route in Hertfordshire was Service 14, which started on 3rd May as a commercial operation on Wednesdays from Bassingbourn, The Mordens and Ashwell to Stevenage. A few days earlier (on 30th April) there had been yet another revival, when the Tuesday Stapleford - Sawston - Saffron Walden link was restored. It had run until June 1970 as Service 23, but that number was now unavailable and it reappeared as Service 16. A Sunday extension took Service 9 over its weekday route as far as Ickleton and on through to Saffron Walden, over the route of Cambus 112, while additional fast journeys continued to operate from Cambridge to Duxford Museum on Special Flying Days.

The restoration of long-gone rural bus services was very welcome, and it was encouraging to see Premier Travel re-appearing on routes into Royston and Saffron Walden, especially after cutbacks in Haverhill. The new and revived bus services normally provided one round trip for shoppers on market days, but air travellers had far more choice. The eight daily coaches on Service 79 (Cambridge - Stansted - Heathrow - Gatwick) were now augmented by five more. These ran as Service 78 via Royston, Letchworth, Hitchin and Stevenage, the combined services giving an impressive hourly service for much of the day, which was very far-removed from the early days of Service 79, with all its restrictions. Service 38 continued to provide a two-hourly service from Haverhill and Victoria to Stansted, although the short Victoria - Stansted

Sunday journeys were withdrawn in May. Service 4 reappeared, along with Service 72, the latter in its traditional Haverhill - Bournemouth form.

National Express changes included a new Service 350 from Liverpool and Manchester, which followed the 351 route either to Great Yarmouth, or to Colchester and Clacton. Further alterations came in October, when a daily Cambridge - Hereford journey was provided on Service 305, but this was not a Premier operation. Service 351 disappeared, largely replaced by the new 350 although passengers for Whitehaven and the Lake District now had to change in Birmingham or Preston. Premier retained twelve National diagrams, the coaches appearing on Services 305, 350 and 747, as well as on the 307/308 from Birmingham to King's Lynn and Great Yarmouth.

Another notable transfer from County was that of MPJ210L, a Leyland Atlantean converted to open-top. It appeared on a new Cambridge City Tour operated jointly with Cambus, which started on 26th May, competing with a similar service introduced just over a year earlier by Guide Friday. From 1st August the Atlantean also appeared on a service to Duxford Museum, but neither operation was very successful, and the bus was returned to County in September. Guide Friday have continued to operate their tour on an all-year-round basis. Inter-company transfers continued in September, with the loan of two Plaxton-bodied Tigers in Green Line livery from County (B269/282KPF). It was intended to transfer these coaches to the Premier fleet, but after two months they returned to Sovereign. Two AEC Reliances (JVE370P and NEB348R) were loaned to County at Hoddesdon, where they worked alongside Duple-bodied Tiger A137RMJ which had been transferred in April. An interesting departure at the end of the year was that of Volvo/Van Hool D849KVE, which was returned off lease, although the rest of this distinctive batch remained in service.

By May 1989 relations with Cambus had improved. A joint excursion programme was advertised, and a Cambridge City Tour was briefly operated using this Leyland Atlantean borrowed from County Bus & Coach. The bus also appeared on a special service to Duxford Museum, but the open-top operations were not particularly successful and the Atlantean returned to County in September. It is seen here at Premier Park with the surviving Fleetline, which by then had become rather battered by overhanging trees. *G R Mills*

Further repaints into the grey and blue livery were carried out, and a batch of the new Volvo/Plaxton Expressliners had been ordered, for delivery early in 1990. The future again looked bright for a company which two years earlier seemed to be about to pass into history. The only apparent difficulty lay with Premier Park, which had been retained by the main Premier Travel Group, and had to be vacated by the summer of 1990. The Haverhill outstation saw several changes, and moved early in the new year from Falconer Road to the Samuel Ward School. Premier Travel was not the only company to have seen upheavals; from 10th September 1989, Cambus Holdings Ltd transferred its Peterborough operations to the new Viscount Bus & Coach Company, and from 8th January Viscount joined Premier and Cambus on Service X2 (Peterborough - Bury St Edmunds). Now branded 'Speedline', it was also diverted via St Ives. Until March 1990 Premier and Cambus provided a Sunday service on the route for Cambridgeshire County Council, which retained the former service number (792) and continued to reach Ipswich.

January also saw the loan of two ECW-bodied Tigers from Cambus, following the return of the Southdown Leopards; WEX826/828X were in National livery and stayed until March. By then all fourteen of the new Volvo/Plaxton Expressliners had been delivered, registered G369-382REG. As National Express renewed service contracts, operators were required to equip their fleets with the new standard coaches with their distinctive, windowless rear profiles incorporating huge 'double-N' logos. National Express was the only fleetname displayed, so that Premier's largest-ever batch of new coaches did not display the attractive grey and blue fleetname device. The ruling also applied to older National-liveried coaches, and the Premier vinyls quickly disappeared. One of the Expressliners (G382REG) appeared in the British Coach Rally, which took place in Southampton for the first time.

The Expressliners saw off E358/9NEG (transferred to Sovereign) and KUB546V (returned to West Yorkshire), along with ex-Yelloway Tiger FWH37Y and Reliances PCE601/602R. The new vehicles lacked individuality but there were still plenty of grey and blue coaches to be seen, and Services 78/79 saw even more increases from 1st April. The number of daily departures went up to eighteen, with Service 78 now calling additionally at Luton Airport, although it no longer served Stevenage. A reduced timetable was introduced on Service 38, although there were still four coaches on weekdays (including one from Linton) and three on Sundays. A joint Cambus/Premier excursion programme was again offered.

Premier Travel had survived the rigours of coach and bus deregulation and after all the upheavals things were settling down again. Several of the National Express services provided reminders of the pioneering days when Mr Lainson's blue coaches were building up a successful long-distance network, and Cambridge was now a key interchange point with regular departures throughout the day (and night in the case of the airport services). The summer services were due to start on 20th May, and Service 72 continued the tradition of a direct Haverhill - Bournemouth service when it reappeared on that date. What came as a complete surprise to many people was that the AJS Group had decided to sell most of its south of England operations, including a large part of Premier Travel Services. Less surprising was that Cambus Holdings Ltd was the successful bidder.

POSTSCRIPT

On 20th May 1990, a great bus and coach company was divided up. A well-known independent enterprise seemed to have ended after more than 54 years, although the new operator of the vehicles carrying the Premier Travel fleetname was also now in the private sector.

The most obvious change was on the bus routes. These were all transferred to Cambus, whose standard buses (mostly Leyland Nationals) replaced Premier's coaches. The Cambus vehicles initially operated "on hire to Premier Travel", and very unfamiliar machines now made their way along remote country roads, reaching villages never previously served by Eastern Counties or its successor.

The change was less obvious to begin with on the coach side. The vehicles which passed to Cambus Holdings Ltd consisted of the Expressliners, two Volvos, most of the Tigers, all the Leopards, all but one of the remaining Reliances, and the Fleetline. Thirteen school services were transferred, along with the remaining contracts operated for Philips (formerly Pye) and others. The AECs were delicensed at the end of June, although two of them became training vehicles (RVE652S for Cambus and NEB348R for Viscount, the latter initially re-registered 46CNG). The Leopards lasted until the end of September.

Cambus Holdings Ltd took over all Premier Travel's National Express operations and combined them with those of Cambus, adopting Premier Travel Services as a fleetname for all its Cambridge-based coach operations. The Cambus coach fleet, including four more Expressliners, passed to the new Premier Travel Services, and another new livery appeared, with two-tone blue and grey on a white base in the style of the Viscount company. The first coach to be repainted was Leyland Tiger C332PEW.

However, not everything went to Cambus Holdings Ltd, for the AJS Group kept the lucrative airport routes (Services 78/79), along with Service 72 (Haverhill - Bournemouth) and Service 38 (now Haverhill - London, the Linton section having ceased). AJS also retained the grey and blue livery, along with the logo, but what seemed at a glance to be Premier Travel coaches were now operating for Cambridge Coach Services Ltd, the CAMBRIDGE fleetname (in PREMIER style) having been in use since early April on publicity material. Service 4 disappeared, but Cambridge Coach Services kept 44 per cent of Premier's express mileage, and retained the 1990 Excursion and Tour programme. Most of the initial Cambridge Coach Services fleet was quite new, comprising sixteen Volvos, two of the original batch of Tigers, and a solitary Reliance.

The last batch of coaches delivered before the company was split was also the largest, and fourteen of these Volvo/Plaxton Expressliners had entered service by March 1990. Unlike the other coaches in National Express livery they did not feature the silver and blue logos, only the legal lettering revealing that they were owned by Premier Travel. Looking rather anonymous, this one is seen when new in Luton on the daily Cambridge-Paignton journey introduced in 1988. By then all Service 747 journeys followed the original Premier Travel route between Cambridge and Oxford. The route was renumbered 347 in 1993. *G R Mills*

New beginnings. Although at first glance a Premier Travel vehicle, this Van Hool-bodied Volvo shows off the CAMBRIDGE fleetname adopted after the division of Premier Travel Services Ltd in May 1990. Cambridge Coach Services Ltd retained 44 per cent of Premier's express mileage, including the airport services, which now provide an hourly service for much of the day (and night). The coach is seen here on the Service 78 variation from Cambridge to Luton, Heathrow and Gatwick Airports. *G R Mills*

A number of changes soon took place. On 1st July Premier Travel Services took over all Viscount's coaching. Fourteen coaches were transferred, together with Bristol FLF6G open-topper JAH552D, named 'Pride of Peterborough'. On 28th August, Cambus reorganised some of the ex-Premier bus routes. Services 1/2 (Cambridge - Fowlmere - Barley) were numbered 31/32, with Haslingfield now mainly served by a diversion of Cambus 146. Commuter Services 3 (Royston) and 40 (Haverhill) became X3 and X4, with the former styled 'The Royston Flyer'. Service 9 (Cambridge - Duxford) was absorbed by Cambus 103, while the 14 (Bassingbourn - Stevenage) and 16 (Stapleford - Saffron Walden) were withdrawn. The latter was incorporated into Service 22 (Cambridge - Saffron Walden), which was diverted via Sawston, and increased as part of the battle with Millerbus, as the Foxton operator was now known. On Service 44 (Cambridge - Haverhill), the section beyond Fulbourn was withdrawn, replaced by commuter Service X4 and new Service 45, which initially covered all but the Burrough Green - Haverhill section, although Cambus 113 was extended from Haverhill to Kedington. Most journeys on Services 44/45 were converted to minibus operation. Market-day Services 49, 55 and 56 were absorbed into other routes. Cambus continued to operate the tendered services, although the operation of the Hertfordshire routes was short-lived. After a few months the tenders were all re-awarded to C G Myall of Bassingbourn, whose vehicles appear on numerous other council-supported services in the area. Cambus vehicles have also now disappeared from the tendered routes in Cambridgeshire and Essex.

THE MID-NINETIES SCENE

Five years on, a visit to the Cambridge area evoked many memories. Cambus still operated Services X3, X4, 31, 32, 44 and 45 into Cambridge, while Service 22 had become a Millerbus operation, Cambus having acquired its competitor from 14th February 1992. Essex Services 11 and 29 were also operated by Millerbus for a while, but these passed to Viceroy Coaches. Millerbus also operated Essex Service 18 (Haverhill - Saffron Walden), but the few remaining journeys later reverted to Hedingham Omnibuses. Commercial operations by Hedingham include most of Service 59 (Haverhill - Audley End Station), and a town service in Saffron Walden, with timings just ahead of the Essex tendered operations (Services 14/34), which are also now provided by Viceroy. Haverhill and Saffron Walden are also linked by Service 38, which is still operated by Cambridge Coach Services, though now reduced to two daily coaches. The route has been extended to give a through service from Cambridge to London, with local fares available between Cambridge and Bishop's Stortford.

Another former Premier Travel route operated for Essex County Council is Service 10 (Chrishall - Bishop's Stortford). This was restored in September 1993, and is worked by Myall's Coaches, who have retained all the former Premier routes in Hertfordshire, and continue to provide Services 17 (Bishop's Stortford - Puckeridge circular), 23, 24, 25, 26, 27,28, 41, 42 and 43. Operations are capably handled by Andrew Weir, also a former Premier man, and some of Myall's Almex tickets even show Premier Travel as the operator! In Royston, Myall's vehicles meet Richmond's minibuses, which work the town services (16 and 17). Most of Haverhill town services (now H1 to H7) are still provided by Cambus and Neal's, with some participation by Steeds Minicoaches. The newest operator to appear on former Premier Travel routes is Andrew's Coaches of Sawston, run by a member of the Miller family. Andrew's operate

Cambridgeshire Services 46 (Linton - Newmarket), and the very roundabout 139 (Foxton - Sawston - Royston).

Premier Travel Services retained the Eastline/Speedline route (now numbered X51) until 4th January 1994, when it passed to United Counties as part of their Coachlinks network. The Newmarket section ceased, and it now provides a fast Cambridge - Peterborough link. The coaches of Premier Travel Services remain as active as ever, and many new vehicles have joined the fleet, some with the distinction of individual names. The depot at Kilmaine Close remains in use, although the National Express operations transferred to the Cowley Road premises in March 1994. A few 'genuine' Premier coaches survive, and some received yet another new livery style during 1993. WEB410/411T now carry Millers of Cambridge lettering, but WEB406-408T still display Premier Travel Services fleetnames, even though they belong to a company very different from the one which began operations in January 1936. A reminder of the pre-1973 Premier blue livery is provided by preserved Harrington-bodied AEC Reliance HLP10C. This immaculate coach is now in the care of Geoff Cochrane, and is a regular rally attender. The Premier Travel name is also kept alive by the travel agencies.

As for the rural depots, Funston's Coaches continue to operate from Chrishall, although some of the buildings have been demolished. A car showroom occupies the site at Harston, a doctors' surgery has been built at Haverhill, with new housing at West Wratting where life-expired buses and coaches used to await disposal. Part of the Godmanchester site has become a cemetery, but a derelict building survives on the adjacent waste ground, which is still owned by Premier Travel Holdings Ltd.

The operations of Cambridge Coach Services (now part of Blazefield Holdings Ltd) have returned to King's Hedges Road after a period at Waterbeach, and have also received new coaches. The company is still "linking Cambridge to the world", with day and night journeys on Services 77/78/79. From May to October 1993, coaches called at Cambridge railway station following the run-down of train services to Stansted Airport from the north. As well as the airport routes and London Service 38, Cambridge Coach Services still operate Service 72 from Cambridge to Bournemouth on summer Saturdays, although the Haverhill section ran for the last time in 1993. Several notable new services have also been introduced, as National Express reduced the number of coaches between Cambridge and Oxford on Service 347 (formerly 747), Cambridge Coach Services started its own service between the University cities in 1992. Service 75 now offers six daily journeys via Amersham and High Wycombe as well as giving further coaches to Stansted Airport. This route revived two earlier traditions: for a while it too called at Cambridge railway station, while the name 'Inter-Varsity Link' provides another reminder of Premier Travel's great post-war expansion. King's College still appears on the company logo, and several coaches have also been named after other Cambridge colleges, recalling those far-off days in the 1930s, when a group of undergraduates decided to start a bus company...

In the competitive and deregulated 1990s, the regular comings and goings of the grey and blue coaches at Drummer Street provide an attractive accompaniment to the white National vehicles, and give a good idea of what might have been had Premier Travel's other express services remained outside the National Express network. The independent enterprise continues!

LIST OF VEHICLES OPERATED 1936-1990

(Original fleet numbers are shown, some of which were subsequently changed)

Fleet No.	Reg No.	Chassis	Body	Date In	Date Out	Previous Owner	New
48	VE3002	Reo	??? -14-	1/36	2/38	Harston & District	1930
6	VE4993	Gilford 1680T	Beadle C30F	1/36	7/45	Harston & District	1931
50	VE8761	Gilford AS6	??? -20-	1/36	9/44	Harston & District	1933
8	WG334	Gilford 1680T	Wycombe C32F	1/36	-/43	Harston & District	1931
54	YE4390	ADC 419	LGOC C28F	1/36	12/36	Royal Blue, Cambridge	1927
52	VE919	Maudslay	??? C32-	1/36	12/36	Royal Blue, Cambridge	1929
4	BVE668	Bedford WTB	Duple C25F	12/36	12/52	New	
47	VE855	Reo Pullman	??? B26-	5/37	5/38	Harston & District	1929
9	WG1284	Gilford 1680T	Wycombe C32F	3/37	7/44	W. Alexander	1932
16	CCE568	Dennis Lancet 2	Duple C35F	5/37	5/57	New	
1	HX3464	Gilford AS6	Duple C20F	6/38	11/48	Crouch End, London N8	1931
55	TM8465	Gilford 1680T	Strachan C30F	6/38	8/42	Eastern National	1931
9	ECE879	Bedford OWB	Duple UB32F	9/43	8/58	New	
10	ECE948	Bedford OWB	Duple UB32F	1/44	8/58	New	
11	EER242	Bedford OWB	Duple UB32F	9/44	12/59	New	
6	MO8513	Dennis F	Duple C30F	9/44	1/50	Windsorian, Windsor	1927
7	TF1555	Leyland Tiger TS1	Alexander C32F	2/45	9/51	Rowe, Cudworth	1930
14	EER570	Bedford OWB	Duple B32F	8/45	12/59	New	
8	WG1273	Gilford 1680T	Wycombe C32F	9/45	11/48	Weeden, Chrishall	1932
2	BCE372	Albion 530	Watson C20F	9/45	5/49	Weeden, Chrishall	1935
3	CUR921	Albion PK114	Waveney C26F	9/45	1/52	Weeden, Chrishall	1937
11	CVE424	Bedford WTB	Duple C20F	9/45	6/55	Weeden, Chrishall	1938
13	ECE794	Bedford OWB	Mulliner UB32F	9/45	11/47	Weeden, Chrishall	1943
12	EER99	Bedford OWB	Duple UB32F	9/45	9/60	Weeden, Chrishall	1944
15	CVE12	Dennis Lancet 2	Duple C32F	9/45	7/58	Weeden, Chrishall	1938
19	WG329	Gilford 1680T	Wycombe C32F	5/46	12/50	Gill, Godmanchester	1931
20	JF2725	Bedford WLB	Duple B20F	5/46	2/48	Gill, Godmanchester	1932
21	EW7332	Bedford WLB	Duple B20F	5/46	2/48	Gill, Godmanchester	1932
18	MJ2154	Gilford Hera	Strachan C32F	5/46	11/48	Gill, Godmanchester	1930
17	AG6221	Leyland Tiger TS1	Alexander C33F	7/46	2/52	Western SMT	1931
22	GJ5124	Leyland Tiger TS3	United C28F	8/46	7/48	Mascot, Norwich	1930
23	FER241	Bedford OB	Duple B32F	2/47	2/61	New	
6	FD9601	Leyland Cub SKP3	???? C26R	5/47	9/50	Drayton, Barley	1935
19	WG1286	Gilford 1680T	Wycombe C31F	5/47	7/49	Drayton, Barley	1932
24	ENK387	Dennis Lancet 2	Duple C32F	5/47	5/48	Drayton, Barley	1938
25	JH4429	Gilford AS6	???? C20F	5/47	11/48	Drayton, Barley	1932
26	DRO972	Dennis Pike	Duple C20F	5/47	11/54	Drayton, Barley	1938
27	CWD840	Bedford WTB	Duple C26F	5/47	2/49	Drayton, Barley	1939
28	BFD955	Bedford WTB	???? C26F	5/47	2/49	Drayton, Barley	1937
29	BAJ161	Bedford WTB	Plaxton C26F	5/47	9/57	Drayton, Barley	1938
30	GCE655	Daimler CVD6	W&M C33F	1/48	2/61	New	
31	GCE654	Daimler CVD6	W&M C33F	1/48	10/60	New	
38	GCE422	Bedford OB	Mulliner B31F	1/48	11/63	New	
36	BU7601	Leyland Titan TD2	EE H28/26R	4/48	4/52	Oldham Corporation	1932
39	GER422	Bedford OB	Duple C29F	6/48	-/63	New	
37	DW6942	Leyland Titan TD1	Leyland L24/24R	8/48	8/49	Red & White, Chepstow	1930
38	DW6944	Leyland Titan TD1	Leyland L24/24R	8/48	7/50	Red & White, Chepstow	1930
40	GER217	Dennis Lancet J3	Duple C35F	8/48	-/63	New	
32	GER140	Leyland Tiger PS1/1	W&M C33F	10/48	9/61	New	
33	GER141	Leyland Tiger PS1/1	W&M C33F	1/49	1/61	New	
34	GER834	Leyland Tiger PS1/1	W&M C33F	1/49	1/62	New	
35	GER835	Leyland Tiger PS1/1	W&M C33F	4/49	4/62	New	
37	JY6739	Leyland Titan TD4c	Weymann L24/24R	4/49	7/54	Plymouth Corporation	1936
76	AOP777	Daimler COG5	BRCW H30/24R	10/49	10/50	Long, West Wratting	1935
77	JO8456	AEC Regent I	Weymann H28/24R	12/49	5/52	Long, West Wratting	1933
78	JO8663	AEC Regent I	Park Royal H28/24R	12/49	10/52	Long, West Wratting	1934
60	GV2405	Gilford Hera	Duple C32R	12/49	11/50	Burgoin, Haverhill	1934
62	ACF272	Bedford OB	Duple C29F	12/49	2/64	Burgoin, Haverhill	1946
63	ACF672	Bedford OB	Thurgood C29F	12/49	2/61	Burgoin, Haverhill	1946
64	AGV194	Bedford OB	Duple C29F	12/49	2/64	Burgoin, Haverhill	1947
65	BGV261	Bedford OB	Duple C29F	12/49	6/64	Burgoin, Haverhill	1948
66	BGV401	AEC Regal III	Willowbrook DP35F	12/49	-/63	Burgoin, Haverhill	1949
67	BGV719	Bedford OB	Duple C29F	12/49	6/64	Burgoin, Haverhill	1949
68	CS4326	Leyland Cub SKP2	Burlingham C27F	12/49	????	Burgoin, Haverhill	1935
69	HA9797	Bedford WLB	Bush & Twiddy C20F	12/49	11/51	Burgoin, Haverhill	1934
70	GV5160	Bedford WTB	Duple C26R	12/49	7/57	Burgoin, Haverhill	1937
71	GV9861	Bedford OB	Duple B32F	12/49	10/59	Burgoin, Haverhill	1946

61	GV5552	Bedford WTB	Duple C26R	1/50	-/59	Burgoin, Haverhill	1937
53	GV8751	Bedford OWB	Mulliner UB32F	5/50	8/56	Burgoin, Haverhill	1943
79	HVE36	Dennis Lancet J3	Duple C35F	4/50	-/63	New (ordered by Drayton's)	
80	HVE242	Bedford OB	Duple C29F	4/50	-/64	New	
72	HVE401	Daimler CVD6	W&M FCL27/26RD	4/50	4/64	New	
73	HVE402	Daimler CVD6	W&M FCL27/26RD	6/50	6/66	New	
74	HVE403	Daimler CVD6	W&M FCL27/26RD	7/50	7/66	New	
81	HVE707	Dennis Lancet J3	Duple C35F	5/50	-/64	New	
82	JY3642	Leyland Titan TD3	Weymann L24/24R	11/51	8/55	Plymouth Corporation	1934
83	ANT471	Dennis Lancet 2	Dennis C35F	1/52	7/58	Salopia, Whitchurch	1938
84	FTD195	Daimler CWG5	Brush UL27/28R	5/52	8/56	Haslingden Corporation	1943
85	CVP138	AEC Regent I 0661	Metro-Cammell H30/24R	10/52	7/57	Harvey, Cottenham	1937
86	BGA60	Leyland Titan TD5	Weymann H30/26R	1/53	2/56	Glasgow Corporation	1937
87	HWA277	Leyland Titan TD7	NCB H30/26R	7/53	3/57	Sheffield Corporation	1942
88	BLH887	AEC Regent I 0661	LPTB H29/23F	11/53	4/56	London Transport	1935
89	CXX380	AEC Regent I 0661	LPTB H30/26R	11/53	11/59	London Transport	1936
90	DLU225	AEC Regent I 0661	LPTB H30/25R	2/54	12/57	London Transport	1937
91	DGX285	AEC Regent I 0661	LPTB H30/26R	3/54	10/56	London Transport	1936
92	DLU227	AEC Regent I 0661	LPTB H30/26R	6/54	11/56	London Transport	1937
93	DLU242	AEC Regent I 0661	LPTB H30/25R	6/54	9/55	London Transport	1937
94	ELP138	AEC Regent I 0661	LPTB H30/26R	11/54	2/58	London Transport	1937
95	DYL827	AEC Regent I 0661	LPTB H30/26R	12/54	12/57	London Transport	1937
96	DGX195	AEC Regent I 0661	LPTB H30/26R	7/55	2/58	London Transport	1937
97	CCX651	Daimler CWA6	Duple UL27/28R	11/55	11/58	Huddersfield Corporation	1944
98	CCX662	Daimler CWA6	Brush UL27/28R	12/55	11/60	Huddersfield Corporation	1944
99	DGG916	Daimler CWA6	NCME UH30/26R	9/55	8/57	Glasgow Corporation	1944
100	GNN664	Daimler CWA6	Duple UH30/26R	10/55	10/58	Mansfield District	1945
101	GNN665	Daimler CWA6	Duple UH30/26R	10/55	8/58	Mansfield District	1945

The Bishop's Stortford services were once very busy, and relief buses were needed on market days. Former Huddersfield Daimler CWA6 GNN665 shows the stark lines of its utility body as it waits to leave with a healthy load. Behind is former Southdown Guy Arab GUF131, with neither bus giving any clues to its eventual destination. *A D Packer*

102	GUF136	Guy Arab II	NCME UH28/26R	3/57	1/62	Southdown		1944
103	GUF157	Guy Arab II	NCME UH30/26R	3/57	2/62	Southdown		1944
104	GUF131	Guy Arab II	NCME UH28/26R	3/57	2/62	Southdown		1944
105	GUF190	Guy Arab II	NCME UH28/26R	5/57	2/62	Southdown		1944
106	GUF130	Guy Arab II	NCME UH28/26R	6/57	3/62	Southdown		1944
107	GUF394	Guy Arab II	Weymann UH30/26R	9/57	10/61	Southdown		1945
108	CDR756	Guy Arab II	Roe UL27/28R	1/58	1/62	Plymouth Corporation		1944
109	GUF173	Guy Arab II	Weymann UH30/26R	1/58	1/62	Southdown		1944
110	CDR750	Guy Arab II	Roe UL27/28R	5/58	2/62	Plymouth Corporation		1944
111	CDR748	Guy Arab II	Roe UL27/28R	5/58	3/62	Plymouth Corporation		1944
112	HOM677	Dennis Lancet J3	Duple C35F	6/58	6/64	Price, Broughton Astley		1948
113	KGY940	Dennis Lancet J3	Duple C35F	8/58	-/63	Popular, London E16		1950
114	UVE333	AEC Reliance 2MU3RV	Burlingham C41F	7/59	7/70	New		
115	GKP656	Daimler CWA6	Weymann H30/26R (1951)	6/59	6/65	Maidstone & District		1944
116	GKP266	Daimler CWA6	Weymann H30/26R (1951)	6/59	11/61	Maidstone & District		1943
117	GKP262	Daimler CWA6	Weymann H30/26R (1951)	6/59	6/65	Maidstone & District		1943
118	BWY986	Bristol K5G	ECW L27/28R (1949)	11/59	11/65	West Yorkshire		1937
119	BWY993	Bristol K5G	ECW L27/28R (1949)	12/59	-/64	West Yorkshire		1937
120	BWY979	Bristol K5G	ECW L27/28R (1949)	12/59	8/67	West Yorkshire		1937
121	BTR312	Bristol K5G	ECW L27/28R (1949)	5/60	2/65	Hants & Dorset		1938
122	XMT54	AEC Regal IV 9821E	Burlingham C41C	6/60	9/64	Valliant, London W5		1952
123	XMT55	AEC Regal IV 9821E	Burlingham C41C	6/60	-/66	Valliant, London W5		1952
124	XMT56	AEC Regal IV 9821E	Burlingham C41C	6/60	11/66	Valliant, London W5		1952
125	CWX667	Bristol K5G	ECW L27/28R (1949)	11/60	11/67	West Yorkshire		1938
126	BWY988	Bristol K5G	ECW L27/28R (1949)	11/60	2/65	West Yorkshire		1937
127	FWX821	Bristol K5G	ECW L27/28R (1949)	12/60	-/64	West Yorkshire		1948
128	BWY985	Bristol K5G	ECW L27/28R (1949)	12/60	12/64	West Yorkshire		1948
129	TMM829	Bedford OB	Duple C29F	3/61	2/64	Star Hire, Surbiton		1950
130	GFU700	Bedford OB	Duple C29F	4/61	2/64	Farmery, Pontefract		1950
131	MKL51	Bedford OB	Duple C29F	5/61	3/64	Star Hire, Surbiton		1950
132	138EMF	AEC Reliance MU3RV	Burlingham C41F	5/61	3/68	Alexandra, Enfield		1955
133	XHA731	AEC Reliance MU3RV	Burlingham C41F	5/61	1/70	Morris, Bearwood		1955

Although purchased for long-distance work, these Burlingham-bodied AEC Reliance coaches were regular performers on Premier Travel's rural bus services during the late 1960s. The scene is Heydon, on the Essex/Hertfordshire border between Chrishall and the market town of Royston. This particular coach was purchased from Morris of Bearwood in 1961, and was withdrawn nine years later. *C W Routh*

134	KKK863	Bristol K6A	Weymann H30/26R	10/61	10/65	Maidstone & District	1948
135	LKT998	Bristol L6A	ECW B35R	10/61	6/64	Maidstone & District	1950
136	KKK859	Bristol K6A	Weymann H30/26R	10/61	10/65	Maidstone & District	1948
141	LKT993	Bristol L6A	ECW B35R	11/61	12/64	Maidstone & District	1950
139	LKT999	Bristol L6A	ECW B35R	11/61	12/64	Maidstone & District	1950
149	LKT984	Bristol L6A	ECW B35R	1/62	12/64	Maidstone & District	1950
137	DCK211	Leyland Titan PD2/3	East Lancs FL27/26RD	1/62	2/72	Ribble	1950
138	DCK212	Leyland Titan PD2/3	East Lancs FL27/26RD	1/62	5/72	Ribble	1950
139	DCK206	Leyland Titan PD2/3	East Lancs FL27/26RD	1/62	8/72	Ribble	1950
140	DCK208	Leyland Titan PD2/3	East Lancs FL27/26RD	1/62	4/73	Ribble	1950
141	DCK205	Leyland Titan PD2/3	East Lancs FL27/26RD	1/62	7/72	Ribble	1950
142	DCK218	Leyland Titan PD2/3	East Lancs FL27/26RD	1/62	7/70	Ribble	1950
143	DCK217	Leyland Titan PD2/3	East Lancs FL27/26RD	1/62	4/73	Ribble	1950
144	DCK215	Leyland Titan PD2/3	East Lancs FL27/26RD	2/62	7/72	Ribble	1950
145	DCK214	Leyland Titan PD2/3	East Lancs FL27/26RD	2/62	5/72	Ribble	1950
146	DCK204	Leyland Titan PD2/3	East Lancs FL27/26RD	3/62	9/72	Ribble	1950
150	XHN573	AEC Reliance MU3RV	Burlingham C41F	6/62	6/69	Scott's Greys, Darlington	1955
151	201EMP	AEC Reliance MU3RV	Burlingham C41F	6/62	6/69	Valliant, London W5	1955
152	UAF281	AEC Reliance MU3RA	Burlingham C41F	5/63	6/69	Hawkey, Newquay	1955
153	772EMU	AEC Reliance MU3RV	Burlingham C41F	5/63	12/68	Drew, Canterbury	1955
154	199EMP	AEC Reliance MU3RV	Burlingham C41F	5/63	5/69	Valliant, London W5	1955
155	75TML	AEC Reliance 2MU3RA	Burlingham C41F	5/63	5/73	Valliant, London W5	1959
156	76TML	AEC Reliance 2MU3RA	Burlingham C41F	5/63	5/73	Valliant, London W5	1959
157	86UME	AEC Reliance 2MU3RA	Burlingham C41F	5/63	4/73	Valliant, London W5	1959
158	UDK314	AEC Reliance 2MU3RV	Burlingham C41F	12/63	6/71	Yelloway, Rochdale	1959
159	UDK313	AEC Reliance 2MU3RA	Burlingham C41F	12/63	5/71	Yelloway, Rochdale	1959
160	ROC161	AEC Reliance MU3RV	Burlingham C41F	2/64	2/68	Stockland, Birmingham	1955
161	LUC202	AEC Regal IV 9821LT	Metro-Cammell B35F	5/64	7/69	London Transport	1951
162	LUC203	AEC Regal IV 9821LT	Metro-Cammell B35F	2/64	8/67	London Transport	1951
163	LUC204	AEC Regal IV 9821LT	Metro-Cammell B35F	3/64	7/69	London Transport	1951
164	LUC206	AEC Regal IV 9821LT	Metro-Cammell B35F	2/64	12/68	London Transport	1951
165	LUC207	AEC Regal IV 9821LT	Metro-Cammell B35F	3/64	7/69	London Transport	1951
166	LUC208	AEC Regal IV 9821LT	Metro-Cammell B35F	3/64	3/70	London Transport	1951
167	LUC209	AEC Regal IV 9821LT	Metro-Cammell B35F	2/64	7/69	London Transport	1951
168	LUC211	AEC Regal IV 9821LT	Metro-Cammell B35F	3/64	7/69	London Transport	1951
169	AVE444B	AEC Reliance 2U3RA	Alexander C49F	6/64	6/78	New	
170	AVE555B	AEC Reliance 2U3RA	Alexander C49F	6/64	10/78	New	
171	83UME	AEC Reliance 2MU3RA	Burlingham C41F	6/64	12/72	Valliant, London W5	1959
172	85UME	AEC Reliance 2MU3RA	Burlingham C41F	6/64	5/73	Valliant, London W5	1959
173	LUC225	AEC Regal IV 9821LT	Metro-Cammell B35F	1/65	11/69	Hume, Hockley	1951
174	MLL519	AEC Regal IV 9821LT	Metro-Cammell B39F	12/64	5/69	London Transport	1952
175	LYF448	AEC Regal IV 9821LT	Metro-Cammell B39F	1/65	7/69	London Transport	1952
176	MLL795	AEC Regal IV 9821LT	Metro-Cammell B39F	1/65	9/69	London Transport	1952
177	MLL819	AEC Regal IV 9821LT	Metro-Cammell B39F	12/64	5/71	London Transport	1952
178	UDK311	AEC Reliance 2MU3RV	Burlingham C41F	1/65	5/71	Yelloway, Rochdale	1959
179	UDK312	AEC Reliance 2MU3RV	Burlingham C41F	1/65	5/71	Yelloway, Rochdale	1959
180	DCE800C	AEC Reliance 2U3RA	Alexander C49F	8/65	4/79	New	
181	DCE801C	AEC Reliance 2U3RA	Alexander C49F	6/65	4/79	New	
182	MDK916	AEC Reliance MU3RV	Burlingham C41F	12/65	12/68	Yelloway, Rochdale	1955
183	MDK917	AEC Reliance MU3RV	Burlingham C41F	12/65	12/68	Yelloway, Rochdale	1955
184	MDK918	AEC Reliance MU3RV	Burlingham C41F	12/65	12/68	Yelloway, Rochdale	1955
185	FCE132D	AEC Reliance 2U3RA	Alexander C49F	6/66	1/80	New	
186	FCE133D	AEC Reliance 2U3RA	Alexander C49F	6/66	10/79	New	
187	DCK219	Leyland Titan PD2/3	East Lancs FL27/22RD	11/66	10/72	Reliance, Newbury	1950
188	GER501E	AEC Reliance 6U3ZR	Alexander C49F	5/67	11/79	New	
189	GER502E	AEC Reliance 6U3ZR	Alexander C49F	5/67	11/79	New	
190	KCN913	AEC Reliance 2HMU3RA	Harrington C37F	12/68	8/74	Northern General	1960
191	KCN916	AEC Reliance 2HMU3RA	Harrington C37F	12/68	12/73	Northern General	1960
192	KCN917	AEC Reliance 2HMU3RA	Harrington C37F	12/68	8/74	Northern General	1960
193	KCN919	AEC Reliance 2HMU3RA	Harrington C37F	12/68	12/73	Northern General	1960
194	KCN920	AEC Reliance 2HMU3RA	Harrington C37F	12/68	8/74	Northern General	1960
195	LJE991G	AEC Reliance 6U3ZR	Alexander C53F	5/69	2/80	New	
196	LJE992G	AEC Reliance 6U3ZR	Alexander C53F	5/69	7/80	New	
197	VDV797	AEC Reliance MU3RA	Metro-Cammell B41F	7/69	9/76	Devon General	1957
198	VDV805	AEC Reliance MU3RA	Metro-Cammell B41F	7/69	7/75	Devon General	1957
199	VDV796	AEC Reliance MU3RA	Metro-Cammell B41F	8/69	8/76	Devon General	1957
200	VDV803	AEC Reliance MU3RA	Metro-Cammell B41F	8/69	8/75	Devon General	1957
201	VDV794	AEC Reliance MU3RA	Metro-Cammell B41F	9/69	9/76	Devon General	1957
202	VDV806	AEC Reliance MU3RA	Metro-Cammell B41F	10/69	10/75	Devon General	1957
203	VDV795	AEC Reliance MU3RA	Metro-Cammell B41F	10/69	11/74	Devon General	1957
204	VDV800	AEC Reliance MU3RA	Metro-Cammell B41F	11/69	11/73	Devon General	1957
205	VDV804	AEC Reliance MU3RA	Metro-Cammell B41F	11/69	1/76	Devon General	1957
206	631WKL	AEC Reliance 2U3RA	Harrington C45F	12/69	3/76	Whyte, Ashford	1963

207	632WKL	AEC Reliance 2U3RA	Harrington C45F	11/70	4/76	Whyte, Ashford		1963
208	633WKL	AEC Reliance 2U3RA	Harrington C45F	11/70	4/76	Whyte, Ashford		1963
209	OVE232J	AEC Reliance 6U3ZR	Alexander C53F	10/70	3/80	New		
210	OVE233J	AEC Reliance 6U3ZR	Alexander C53F	10/70	5/80	New		
211	83BNV	AEC Reliance 2MU3RV	Duple C43F	10/70	12/73	York Bros, Northampton		1962
212	YBD79	AEC Reliance 2MU3RV	Duple C41C	11/70	2/74	York Bros, Northampton		1961
213	YBD80	AEC Reliance 2MU3RV	Duple C41C	11/70	2/74	York Bros, Northampton		1961
214	YBD81	AEC Reliance 2MU3RV	Duple C41C	11/70	2/74	York Bros, Northampton		1961
215	YBD82	AEC Reliance 2MU3RV	Duple C41C	11/70	2/74	York Bros, Northampton		1961
216	NMU6	AEC Reliance 2U3RA	Harrington C51F	2/71	6/75	Valliant-Cronshaw, W5		1963
217	NMU7	AEC Reliance 2U3RA	Harrington C51F	2/71	6/75	Valliant-Cronshaw, W5		1963
218	AMX8A	AEC Reliance 2U3RA	Harrington C51F	2/71	2/79	Valliant-Cronshaw, W5		1963
219	AMX9A	AEC Reliance 2U3RA	Harrington C51F	2/71	6/75	Valliant-Cronshaw, W5		1963
220	BOF854C	AEC Reliance 2U3RA	Harrington C51F	4/71	12/78	Bowen, Birmingham		1965
221	BOF855C	AEC Reliance 2U3RA	Harrington C51F	4/71	12/78	Bowen, Birmingham		1965
222	FMK129B	AEC Reliance 2U3RA	Harrington C51F	5/72	3/76	Rollins, Slough		1964
223	322NJO	AEC Bridgemaster 2B3RA	Park Royal H40/25F	4/72	4/75	City of Oxford		1962
224	326NJO	AEC Bridgemaster 2B3RA	Park Royal H40/25F	5/72	4/77	City of Oxford		1962
225	323NJO	AEC Bridgemaster 2B3RA	Park Royal H40/25F	5/72	5/74	City of Oxford		1962
226	328NJO	AEC Bridgemaster 2B3RA	Park Royal H40/25F	5/72	5/73	City of Oxford		1962
227	319NJO	AEC Bridgemaster 2B3RA	Park Royal H40/25F	5/72	11/74	City of Oxford		1962
228	318NJO	AEC Bridgemaster 2B3RA	Park Royal H40/25F	6/72	6/77	City of Oxford		1962
229	316NJO	AEC Bridgemaster 2B3RA	Park Royal H40/25F	6/72	11/74	City of Oxford		1962
230	317NJO	AEC Bridgemaster 2B3RA	Park Royal H40/25F	7/72	7/75	City of Oxford		1962

The former City of Oxford AEC Bridgemasters were the last traditional double-deckers. They arrived in the summer of 1972, and were mainly confined to the Haverhill town services and to the routes into Cambridge, where 318NJO was photographed soon after entering service. It was one of a pair which later received the new livery, lasting until 1977. No more double-deckers were purchased until 1985.
G R Mills

231	VER261L	AEC Reliance 6U3ZR	Alexander C53F	10/72	3/82	New		See note 1
232	VER262L	AEC Reliance 6U3ZR	Alexander C53F	10/72	8/81	New		See note 1
233	DWD104C	AEC Reliance 2U3RA	Harrington C51F	8/72	10/79	Smith, Tysoe		1965
234	MMX104C	AEC Reliance 2U3RA	Harrington C45F	10/72	2/79	Valliant-Cronshaw, W5		1965
235	MMX103C	AEC Reliance 2U3RA	Harrington C45F	11/72	2/79	Valliant-Cronshaw, W5		1965
236	MMX105C	AEC Reliance 2U3RA	Harrington C45F	11/72	11/78	Valliant-Cronshaw, W5		1965
237	XVE814L	AEC Reliance 6U3ZR	Alexander C49F	6/73	-/86	New		
238	XVE815L	AEC Reliance 6U3ZR	Alexander C49F	6/73	3/85	New		
239	BVO1C	AEC Reliance 4U3RA	Harrington C51F	6/73	1/77	Barton, Chilwell		1965
240	BVO3C	AEC Reliance 4U3RA	Harrington C51F	6/73	10/76	Barton, Chilwell		1965
241	BVO6C	AEC Reliance 4U3RA	Harrington C51F	12/73	12/76	Barton, Chilwell		1965
242	BVO7C	AEC Reliance 4U3RA	Harrington C51F	12/73	12/76	Barton, Chilwell		1965
243	BVO9C	AEC Reliance 4U3RA	Harrington C51F	12/73	2/77	Barton, Chilwell		1965
244	BVO10C	AEC Reliance 4U3RA	Harrington C51F	12/73	2/77	Barton, Chilwell		1965
245	OJE551M	AEC Reliance 6U3ZR	Alexander C49F	5/74	5/85	New		
246	OJE550M	AEC Reliance 6U3ZR	Alexander C49F	5/74	5/85	New		
247	HLP10C	AEC Reliance 2U3RA	Harrington C51F	5/74	4/80	Surrey Motors, Sutton		1965
248	HLP11C	AEC Reliance 2U3RA	Harrington C51F	5/74	4/80	Surrey Motors, Sutton		1965
249	GER913N	AEC Reliance 6U3ZR	Alexander C49F	12/74	3/87	New		
250	GER914N	AEC Reliance 6U3ZR	Alexander C49F	12/74	CHL	New		
251	JVE370P	AEC Reliance 6U3ZR	Plaxton C49F	8/75	CHL	New		
252	JVE371P	AEC Reliance 6U3ZR	Plaxton C49F	8/75	-/88	New		
253	JVE372P	AEC Reliance 6U3ZR	Plaxton C49F	8/75	CHL	New		
254	JVE373P	AEC Reliance 6U3ZR	Plaxton C49F	8/75	8/88	New		
255	KVE906P	AEC Reliance 6U3ZR	Plaxton C49F	1/76	9/88	New		
256	KVE907P	AEC Reliance 6U3ZR	Plaxton C49F	1/76	9/88	New		
257	KVE908P	AEC Reliance 6U3ZR	Plaxton C49F	1/76	6/88	New		
258	KVE909P	AEC Reliance 6U3ZR	Plaxton C49F	1/76	5/88	New		
259	NEB346R	AEC Reliance 6U3ZR	Plaxton C49F	9/76	8/88	New		
260	NEB347R	AEC Reliance 6U3ZR	Plaxton C49F	9/76	CHL	New		
261	NEB348R	AEC Reliance 6U3ZR	Plaxton C49F	10/76	CHL	New		See note 1
262	NEB349R	AEC Reliance 6U3ZR	Plaxton C49F	10/76	CHL	New		
263	WUR856J	AEC Reliance 6U3ZR	Plaxton C50F	3/77	4/82	Grayline, Gosport		1971
264	YUS244J	AEC Reliance 6U3ZR	Plaxton C51F	3/77	4/82	Weir, Dumbarton		1971
265	UAR925M	AEC Reliance 6U3ZR	Plaxton C53F	4/77	10/86	Limebourne, London, SW8		1974
266	URA461K	AEC Reliance 6U3ZR	Plaxton C51F	4/77	1/84	Morris, Pencoed		1971
267	PCE601R	AEC Reliance 6U3ZR	Plaxton C49F	5/77	4/90	New		
268	PCE602R	AEC Reliance 6U3ZR	Plaxton C49F	5/77	4/90	New		
269	UTF478M	AEC Reliance 6U3ZR	Plaxton C53F	7/77	5/87	Cross, Padgate		1974
270	RVE650S	AEC Reliance 6U3ZR	Plaxton C49F	11/77	CHL	New		
271	RVE651S	AEC Reliance 6U3ZR	Plaxton C49F	11/77	11/87	New		
272	RVE652S	AEC Reliance 6U3ZR	Plaxton C49F	6/78	CHL	New		
273	RVE653S	AEC Reliance 6U3ZR	Plaxton C49F	7/78	CHL	New		
274	RVE296S	AEC Reliance 6U3ZR	Plaxton C49F	7/78	CHL	New		
275	RVE297S	AEC Reliance 6U3ZR	Plaxton C49F	7/78	CHL	New		
276	WEB406T	AEC Reliance 6U3ZR	Plaxton C49F	11/78	CHL	New		
277	WEB407T	AEC Reliance 6U3ZR	Plaxton C49F	9/78	CHL	New		
278	WEB408T	AEC Reliance 6U3ZR	Plaxton C49F	2/79	CHL	New		
279	WEB409T	AEC Reliance 6U3ZR	Plaxton C49F	3/79	CCS	New		
280	WEB410T	AEC Reliance 6U3ZR	Plaxton C49F	2/79	CHL	New		
281	WEB411T	AEC Reliance 6U3ZR	Plaxton C49F	3/79	CHL	New		
282	BVA784V	Leyland Leopard PSU3F/4	Plaxton C49F	2/80	CHL	New		
283	BVA785V	Leyland Leopard PSU3F/4	Plaxton C49F	2/80	CHL	New		
284	BVA786V	Leyland Leopard PSU3F/4	Plaxton C49F	3/80	CHL	New		
285	BVA787V	Leyland Leopard PSU3F/4	Plaxton C49F	3/80	CHL	New		
286	BVA788V	Leyland Leopard PSU3F/4	Plaxton C49F	5/80	CHL	New		
287	BVA789V	Leyland Leopard PSU3F/4	Plaxton C49F	5/80	CHL	New		
288	CJE452V	Leyland Leopard PSU3F/4	Plaxton C49F	5/80	CHL	New		
289	CJE453V	Leyland Leopard PSU3F/4	Plaxton C49F	5/80	CHL	New		
290	CJE454V	Leyland Leopard PSU3F/4	Plaxton C49F	5/80	CHL	New		
291	CJE455V	Leyland Leopard PSU3F/4	Plaxton C49F	5/80	CHL	New		
292	VAV254X	Leyland Tiger TRCTL11/3	Plaxton C53F	2/82	CCS	New		
293	VAV255X	Leyland Tiger TRCTL11/3	Plaxton C55F	2/82	1/86	New		
294	VAV256X	Leyland Tiger TRCTL11/3	Plaxton C53F	2/82	CCS	New		
295	VAV257X	Leyland Tiger TRCTL11/3	Plaxton C55F	2/82	CHL	New		
296	VAV258X	Leyland Tiger TRCTL11/3	Plaxton C57F	2/82	CHL	New		
297	FAV564Y	Leyland Tiger TRCTL11/3	Plaxton C53F	3/83	CHL	New		
298	FAV565Y	Leyland Tiger TRCTL11/3	Plaxton C53F	3/83	CHL	New		
299	FAV566Y	Leyland Tiger TRCTL11/3	Plaxton C53F	3/83	CHL	New		
300	FAV567Y	Leyland Tiger TRCTL11/3	Plaxton C51F	3/83	CHL	New		
301	GFL527Y	Leyland Tiger TRCTL11/3	Plaxton C49Ft	5/83	10/88	New		
302	GFL528Y	Leyland Tiger TRCTL11/3	Plaxton C49Ft	5/83	5/88	New		
303	GFL529Y	Leyland Tiger TRCTL11/3	Plaxton C49Ft	5/83	2/89	New		See note 1

304	A638OEG	Leyland Tiger TRCTL11/3R	Plaxton C51Ft	10/83	CHL	New	
305	A695JER	Leyland Tiger TRCTL11/3R	Plaxton C49Ft	7/84	CHL	New	
306	B192JVA	MCW Metroliner HR131/2	MCW C47Ft	11/84	4/88	New	See note 1
307	B244JVA	MCW Metroliner HR131/6	MCW C49Ft	4/85	4/88	New	See note 1
308	B245JVA	MCW Metroliner HR131/6	MCW C49Ft	6/85	4/88	New	See note 1
309	B246JVA	MCW Metroliner HR131/6	MCW C49Ft	6/85	4/88	New	See note 1
310	KJD24P	Leyland Fleetline FE30ALR	Park Royal H45/34F	6/85	5/88	London Transport	1976
311	KJD58P	Leyland Fleetline FE30ALR	Park Royal H45/34F	6/85	5/88	London Transport	1976
312	KJD116P	Leyland Fleetline FE30ALR	Park Royal H45/34F	6/85	CHL	London Transport	1976
313	KUC983P	Leyland Fleetline FE30ALR	MCW H45/34F	6/85	5/88	London Transport	1976
314	KUC989P	Leyland Fleetline FE30ALR	MCW H45/34F	6/85	5/88	London Transport	1976
315	C519KFL	Leyland Royal Tiger	Leyland C49Ft	6/85	4/89	New	
316	SVA924S	Bedford YMT	Plaxton C49D	1/86	1/88	Young, Rampton	1978
317	AEG121Y	Bedford YMT	Plaxton C49Dt	1/86	5/88	Young, Rampton	1982
318	OJD126R	Leyland Fleetline FE30ALR	Park Royal H45/34F	1/86	1/87	Young, Rampton	1977
319	OUC25R	Leyland Fleetline FE30ALR	MCW H45/34F	1/86	1/87	Young, Rampton	1977
320	OUC27R	Leyland Fleetline FE30ALR	MCW H45/34F	1/86	1/87	Young, Rampton	1977
321	OUC28R	Leyland Fleetline FE30ALR	MCW H45/34F	1/86	1/87	Young, Rampton	1977
322	OUC31R	Leyland Fleetline FE30ALR	MCW H45/34F	1/86	1/87	Young, Rampton	1977
323	WAV122X	Mercedes-Benz L608D	Reebur C21F	1/86	9/87	Young, Rampton	1982
324	A132MFL	Mercedes-Benz L608D	Reebur C21F	1/86	9/87	Young, Rampton	1984
325	C325PEW	Mercedes-Benz L307D	Reebur C12F	3/86	CHL	New	
326	C326PEW	Mercedes-Benz L307D	Reebur C12F	3/86	4/89	New	
327	C327PEW	Mercedes-Benz L307D	Reebur C12F	3/86	4/89	New	
328	C328PEW	Leyland Tiger TRCTL11/3RZ	Plaxton C53F	3/86	CHL	New	See note 1
329	C329PEW	Leyland Tiger TRCTL11/3RZ	Plaxton C53F	3/86	CHL	New	
330	C330PEW	Leyland Tiger TRCTL11/3RZ	Plaxton C53F	3/86	CHL	New	
331	C331PEW	Leyland Tiger TRCTL11/3RZ	Plaxton C53F	3/86	3/88	New	
332	C332PEW	Leyland Tiger TRCTL11/3RZ	Plaxton C53F	3/86	CHL	New	
333	C333PEW	Bedford YMPS	Plaxton C30Ft	4/86	4/89	New	
334	FWH37Y	Leyland Tiger TRCTL11/3	Plaxton C53F	3/86	3/90	Yelloway, Rochdale	1983
335	JNM742Y	Leyland Tiger TRCTL11/3RZ	Plaxton C57F	3/86	CHL	The Londoners, SE15	1983
336	JNM743Y	Leyland Tiger TRCTL11/3RZ	Plaxton C57F	3/86	CHL	The Londoners, SE15	1983
337	A832PPP	Leyland Tiger TRCTL11/3R	Plaxton C55F	3/86	CHL	Armchair, Brentford	1984
338	A833PPP	Leyland Tiger TRCTL11/3R	Plaxton C55F	3/86	CHL	Armchair, Brentford	1984
339	A137RMJ	Leyland Tiger TRCTL11/3R	Duple C55F	3/86	4/89	Cavalier, Hounslow	1984
340	B424CMC	Leyland Tiger TRCTL11/3R	Duple C53F	3/86	12/88	Frames, London WC1	1985
341	D524LCS	Volvo B10M-61	Plaxton C53F	8/86	CHL	New	See note 1 1986
	HHY186D	Bristol FLF6G	ECW H38/32F	3/86			See note 2

342	D342KVE	Volvo B10M-61	Van Hool C53F	3/87	CHL	
343	D343KVE	Volvo B10M-61	Van Hool C53F	3/87	CCS	
344	D344KVE	Volvo B10M-61	Van Hool C53F	3/87	CCS	
345	D345KVE	Volvo B10M-61	Van Hool C53F	3/87	CCS	
346	D846KVE	Volvo B10M-61	Van Hool C49Ft	3/87	CCS	
347	D847KVE	Volvo B10M-61	Van Hool C49Ft	3/87	CCS	
348	D848KVE	Volvo B10M-61	Van Hool C49Ft	3/87	CCS	
349	D849KVE	Volvo B10M-61	Van Hool C49Ft	3/87		See note 3
350	D350KVE	Volvo B10M-61	Van Hool C53D	3/87	CCS	
351	D351KVE	Volvo B10M-61	Van Hool C53F	3/87	CCS	
352	E352NEG	Iveco 49.10	Robin Hood DP19F	3/88		See note 4
353	E353NEG	Iveco 49.10	Robin Hood DP19F	3/88		See note 4
354	E354NEG	Iveco 49.10	Robin Hood DP19F	3/88		See note 4
355	E355NEG	Iveco 49.10	Robin Hood DP19F	3/88		See note 4
356	E356NEG	Iveco 49.10	Robin Hood DP19F	3/88		See note 4
357	E357NEG	Iveco 49.10	Robin Hood DP19F	3/88		See note 4
358	E358NEG	Volvo B10M-61	Plaxton C53F	5/88		See note 5
359	E359NEG	Volvo B10M-61	Plaxton C53F	5/88		See note 5
360	E360NEG	Volvo B10M-61	Plaxton C53F	5/88	CCS	
361	E361NEG	Volvo B10M-61	Plaxton C53F	5/88	CCS	
362	E362NEG	Volvo B10M-61	Plaxton C53F	5/88	CCS	
363	E363NEG	Volvo B10M-61	Plaxton C53F	5/88	CCS	
364	E364NEG	Volvo B10M-61	Plaxton C53F	5/88	CCS	
365	E365NEG	Volvo B10M-61	Plaxton C53F	5/88	CCS	
366	E366NEG	Volvo B10M-61	Plaxton C53F	5/88	CCS	
367	E367NEG	Volvo B10M-61	Plaxton C53F	5/88	CCS	
368	KUB546V	Leyland Leopard	Plaxton C49F	4/89		See note 6
369	G369REG	Volvo B10M-61	Plaxton C49Ft	3/90	CHL	
370	G370REG	Volvo B10M-61	Plaxton C49Ft	3/90	CHL	
371	G371REG	Volvo B10M-61	Plaxton C49Ft	3/90	CHL	
372	G372REG	Volvo B10M-61	Plaxton C49Ft	3/90	CHL	
373	G373REG	Volvo B10M-61	Plaxton C49Ft	3/90	CHL	
374	G374REG	Volvo B10M-61	Plaxton C49Ft	3/90	CHL	
375	G375REG	Volvo B10M-61	Plaxton C49Ft	3/90	CHL	
376	G376REG	Volvo B10M-61	Plaxton C49Ft	3/90	CHL	
377	G377REG	Volvo B10M-61	Plaxton C49Ft	3/90	CHL	
378	G378REG	Volvo B10M-61	Plaxton C49Ft	3/90	CHL	
379	G379REG	Volvo B10M-61	Plaxton C49Ft	3/90	CHL	
380	G380REG	Volvo B10M-61	Plaxton C49Ft	3/90	CHL	
381	G381REG	Volvo B10M-61	Plaxton C49Ft	3/90	CHL	
382	G382REG	Volvo B10M-61	Plaxton C49Ft	3/90	CHL	

NOTES ON FLEET LIST

(1)   Subsequent re-registrations VER261L-VWL817; VER262L-558BWL; NEB348R-46CNG; GFL529Y-6087HE;
      B192JVA-XSU912; B245JVA-LDZ3144; B245JVA-LDZ3145; B246JVA-XYK976; C328PEW-HSV195;
      D524LCS-HSV196. D524LCS was originally on long-term loan from Volvo.
(2)   HHY186D was purchased for driver-training ex Nelson, Wickford. New 1966 to Bristol Omnibus Co. Withdrawn 6/88.
(3)   D849KVE returned off lease 12/88.
(4)   E352-357NEG transferred to London Country (North East) 11/88.
(5)   E358/359NEG transferred to Sovereign 3/90.
(6)   KUB546V was ex-West Yorkshire. New 1980. Returned to that operator 3/90.

Standard body codes have been used in this list. Of these, two are no longer in common use: L indicates Lowbridge bodywork,
U indicates Utility bodywork.

Opposite Inheritors of the business – Cambridge Coach Services have more daily departures from
Cambridge than National Express. This Plaxton-bodied Volvo is seen on Service 71 to Stratford, Warwick
and Rugby. This route revives part of a former Premier service of the same number, with three daily
departures to Stratford-on-Avon and Worcester. Its introduction followed the withdrawal of the short-lived
Service 70 to Coventry and Birmingham, which competed with National Express 305. *G R Mills*

ADDITIONAL VEHICLES OPERATED BUT NOT OWNED:
Apart from manufacturers' demonstration vehicles mentioned in the main text, long-term hires took place at various times to cover vehicle shortages. This list shows all vehicles known to have operated on extended loan.

Trimdon MS	EPT940B	Thames Trader 570E	Plaxton C41F	1969
Trimdon MS	EPT942B	Thames Trader 570E	Plaxton C41F	1969
Trimdon MS	EPT943B	Thames Trader 570E	Plaxton C41F	1969
Trimdon MS	EPT944B	Thames Trader 570E	Plaxton C41F	1969
Whiteside, Preston	HJS702	Thames Trader 570E	Duple C41F	1969
Seth, London NW5	416ALC	Thames Trader 570E	Burlingham C41F	1969
BDS, Chiddingfold	4628AD	Thames Trader 570E	Duple C41F	1969
Belmont, Orpington	509BLP	Thames Trader 570F	Duple C41F	1969
Young, Rampton	YEB105T	Bedford YMT	Plaxton C53F	1985-6
Young, Rampton	HEB118X	Bedford YNT	Plaxton C53F	1985-6
Young, Rampton	DFD953B	DAF MB200 DKL	Plaxton C57F	1985-6
Young, Rampton	A129MFL	Dennis Dorchester	Duple C49Ft	1985-6
Young, Rampton	A130MFL	DAF SBR2300 DHS	Jonckheere CH71Ct	1985-6
Young, Rampton	A131MFL	DAF SBR2300 DHS	Jonckheere CH71Ct	1985-6
Young, Rampton	B136AAV	Bedford YNV	Duple C53F	1985-6
Young, Rampton	B137AAV	Leyland Royal Tiger	Plaxton C49Ft	1985-6
Young, Rampton	B140AAV	DAF SB3000 DKSB	Jonckheere C49Ft	1985-6
Yorks Travel	587HMX	Ford R1114	Plaxton C53F	1986
Yorks Travel	TRP72P	Ford R1114	Plaxton C53F	1986
Yorks Travel	AWN655S	Ford R1114	Plaxton C53F	1986
Yorks Travel	BBD484S	Ford R1114	Plaxton C53F	1986
Yorks Travel	DBD61T	Ford R1114	Plaxton C53F	1986
Yorks Travel	LRP22V	Ford R1114	Plaxton C53F	1986
J&R, Teversham	KVS154Y	Bova EL26-581	Bova Europa C49Ft	1986
Fenn, March	VOR578T	Ford R1114	Duple C53F	1986
Fenn, March	KFL101W	Volvo B10M	Duple C53F	1986
Beeston, Hadleigh	BTB685T	AEC Reliance 6U3ZR	Duple C57F	1986
Beeston, Hadleigh	BTB686T	AEC Reliance 6U3ZR	Duple C57F	1986
Beeston, Hadleigh	WED978S	AEC Reliance 6U3ZR	Duple C57F	1986
Beeston, Hadleigh	VRS151L	Daimler Fleetline CRL6	Alexander H45/29D	1986
Bee Line	D827UTF	Ford Transit	Carlyle B16F	1988
Bee Line	D828UTF	Ford Transit	Carlyle B16F	1988
Bee Line	D831UTF	Ford Transit	Carlyle B16F	1988
East Yorkshire	D44OKH	Iveco 49.10	Robin Hood C19F	1988
East Yorkshire	D54OKH	Iveco 49.10	Robin Hood C19F	1988
West Yorkshire	BWY664T	Leyland Leopard PSU3E/4	Plaxton C49F	1988
West Yorkshire	GWU562T	Leyland Leopard PSU3E/4	Plaxton C49F	1988
County	MPJ210L	Leyland Atlantean PDR1A/1Sp	MCW O43/29D	1989
County	B269KPF	Leyland Tiger TRCTL11/2R	Plaxton C49F	1989
County	B282KPF	Leyland Tiger TRCTL11/2R	Plaxton C53F	1989
Southdown	MAP753W	Leyland Leopard PSU3F/4RT	Plaxton DP48F	1989
Southdown	OUP64W	Leyland Leopard PSU3F/4RT	Plaxton DP48F	1989
Cambus	WEX826X	Leyland Leopard PSU3G/4R	ECW C47F	1989
Cambus	WEX828X	Leyland Leopard PSU3G/4R	ECW C47F	1989

ADDITIONAL VEHICLES OWNED BUT NOT OPERATED:

AOP614	Daimler COG5/MCW H30/24R Ex Birmingham Corporation
EK8088	Leyland TD1/Massey L24/24R Ex Red & White (originally Wigan Corporation)
GK5718	Leyland TS3/???? Ex Kearsey, Cheltenham (originally Premier Line, London)
GV406	Reo Pullman/Duple C24- Ex Burgoin, Haverhill
GV2605	Leyland KP3/Duple C24F Ex Burgoin, Haverhill
TJ9275	Leyland LT7/Duple C32R Ex Long, West Wratting
FT5625*	Guy Arab II/NCME H30/36R Ex Tynemouth & District
HD8521*	Leyland PD2/3/Roe H31/25R Ex Yorkshire Woollen District
MTJ721*	AEC Regal IV/Trans-United C41C Ex Rooney, Kilwinning
2524WE*	AEC Bridgemaster/Park Royal H76R Ex Sheffield Corporation

* Purchased for spares